CW01096180

BARRISTERS' CLERKS

To the memory of my mother

John A. Flood

BARRISTERS' CLERKS

THE LAW'S MIDDLEMEN

Manchester
University Press

Published by
Manchester University Press
Oxford Road, Manchester M13 9PL, UK
51 Washington Street, Dover, N.H. 03820, USA

British Library cataloguing in publication data
Flood, John A.
 Barristers' clerks.
 1. Legal assistants—England
 I. Title
 340   KD654
 ISBN 0-7190-0928-6

Library of Congress cataloging in publication data
Flood, John A.
 Barristers' clerks.
 Bibliography: p.
 Includes index.
 1.Legal assistants—Great Britain. I. Title
 KD463.F58 1983   347.42'016   83-912
 ISBN 0-7190-0928-6   344.20716

Printed in Great Britain by
Redwood Burn Ltd, Trowbridge, Wiltshire

CONTENTS

ACKNOWLEDGEMENTS

In producing this book, and the thesis from which it derives, I have incurred many debts. I would like to thank those who generously helped: William L. Twining, Anthony Bradley, Barbara Harrell-Bond, Luke C. Harris, John P. Heinz, Spencer L. Kimball, Geoffrey Wilson and David Farrier.

I am also grateful to the Barristers' Clerks' Association for permission to reproduce their examination papers; and to its officers, past and present, for their assistance and permission to reproduce from their papers: they are Sydney G. Newland, Eric Cooper, C. B. Harrison and Cyril Batchelor. Her Majesty's Stationery Office kindly gave permission to reproduce extracts from the reports of the Royal Commission on Assizes and Quarter Sessions and the Royal Commission on Legal Services. The American Bar Foundation also gave permission to reproduce portions of my article which appeared in 1981 *American Bar Foundation Research Journal* 377. The Lord Chancellor's Office answered my questions with good will. The Social Science Research Council kindly awarded me a Socio-legal Studentship which supported the greater part of the research.

I am grateful to the late Professor Otto Kahn-Freund and C. D. Wickenden, who provided valuable insights and suggestions.

I would also like to thank Ed Atkinson and Caroline Bryant for their support and help.

To those who put the book together I am truly grateful. Jean Fife and Lesley Jones patiently corrected and typed. And Antonia rigorously edited and typed the final draft. It is almost as much her work as it is mine.

My final debt is to the barristers' clerks, necessarily anonymous, who encouraged and assisted me and without whom the study would not have existed.

Chapter 1

BACKGROUND TO THE RESEARCH

In this world there are three 'We's'. The Royal 'We'. The Editorial 'We'. And the Barrister and his Clerk 'We'. And the greatest of these is the Barrister and his Clerk 'We'.[1]

The position of the English barrister's clerk is a unique and disturbing one.[2]

The two quotations represent, perhaps, the extremes of opinion about barristers' clerks. Most of the literature on the topic has been the result of conjecture rather than systematic study. The purpose of this book is to provide that systematic study—and, I hope, a more objective picture than the quotations.

The method I have used to examine the roles and functions of barristers' clerks is more commonly found in anthropology, and sometimes sociology, than law. The study is an ethnography of barristers' clerks. Appendix 1 sets out in greater detail the reasons for selecting this method and provides a context for the research. While the research was in progress the Royal Commission on Legal Services was set up to examine, among other things,

whether any, and if so what, changes are desirable in the public interest in the structure, organisation, training, regulation of and entry to the legal profession, including the arrangements for determining its remuneration, whether from private sources or public funds . . . [Benson (1979): I, vi]

Unfortunately the Royal Commission failed to take the opportunity to carry out any fundamental research on the legal profession, preferring instead to rely on evidence presented by the profession itself, and even this was constrained by the Commission's questionnaire. (See Benson, 1979: I, 4–5.) The Commission gathered large quantities of data but made little use of it to tell us what the legal profession does—which is a pity. Geoffrey Hazard, in discussing the failure of Smigel's study of Wall Street lawyers, pointed out that Smigel did not find out what lawyers actually do, their *raison d'être* (1965: 52–3).

My own study is an attempt to set out what clerks actually do. In it I have explored the relationships they establish with other members of the legal community. Among these three are important: that with the barrister, that with the solicitor, and that with the court list officer. In addition I have analysed the networks that clerks form among themselves.

Little is known about barristers' clerks.[3] And so, in this chapter, I outline the background to the occupation. I start with the structure of the legal profession. Secondly, I show where the clerk appears in it. Thirdly, I briefly describe his tasks. Finally, I sketch an outline of the physical environment and give some details of the history of clerks.

Conventional works on the English legal system portray the profession as divided into three groups: the judiciary, barristers and solicitors.[4] My main concern is with barristers and solicitors. Together they constitute the largest element, numbering approximately 38,000.[5] They do similar work, such as advising, drafting, negotiating and advocacy, but under different conditions. Solicitors administer primary legal care to clients, calling in a barrister if specialist attention is required or if the case is to go to trial.

There are more than 34,000 solicitors. They are situated in most parts of the country, and generally practise in partnerships.[6] Solicitors enjoy two monopolies in their practice. Section 20 of the Solicitors Act, 1974, gives them the right to commence litigation proceedings for others; section 22 of the Act forbids unqualified persons to undertake conveyancing for a fee. Only limited rights of audience in some of the lower courts are granted to solicitors.

Despite the overlap of tasks, including advocacy, barristers are ostensibly the specialists in advocacy. They are a much smaller group than solicitors, numbering around 4,400. Barristers are solo practitioners, although they join together in groups known as chambers to share expenses but not profits.[7] They have a monopoly over the right of audience in the higher courts and so tend to congregate in London, where most High Court matters are heard. In addition, barristers are not permitted to communicate direct with clients, only through solicitors—hence the barrister's clerk is the conduit between the two sides of the profession.[8]

A person who wishes to join the legal profession must decide, while in law school, whether to join an Inn and become a barrister, or the Law Society and become a solicitor. He (or she) cannot do both. From this time, usually during the second year of law school, the student barrister will start to keep terms, that is, eat dinners in hall.[9] After law school a year must be spent in postgraduate education acquiring practical skills such as drafting and advocacy.

The next step is finding a pupilage,[10] and—which is more difficult—a tenancy in chambers.[11] If successful in both endeavours, the new barrister will rely almost entirely on the clerk to build his or her practice. This means the barrister will spend the early years of practice on small cases (lesser criminal matters, traffic offences, landlord-and-tenant disputes, and the like) and drafting pleas and other documents. Much of this work will be sent to the chambers by solicitors the day before trial, or even the day the case is heard. Occasionally a barrister will walk into the clerks' room to be told that there is a case to be dealt with in the next half-hour. Thus the barrister has very little control over the progress of his or her career in the early stages; it all depends on the barrister's clerk.

Essentially the clerk is the middleman, or mediator, between the diverse interests of the legal system, namely those of barristers, solicitors, judges, list officers, and occasionally the client upon whom the system depends. Although these groups are discrete, they are interdependent. But their interdependence does not prevent them from pressing divergent demands that must somehow be resolved into a common aim if the legal process is to function reasonably smoothly. How is this resolution effected? By the clerk—and in so doing he assumes different roles to satisfy the demands, but keeping in mind his own interests.

Broadly, there are three such roles: counsellor, negotiator, and 'fixer'.[12] Perhaps the most important is that of fixer, since the others are variants of it.

While performing these roles the clerk carries out a number of tasks. The main ones are negotiating his barristers' fees and collecting them, obtaining work for his barristers, supervising their and the chambers' accounts, helping to schedule cases and checking the daily court lists for his barristers and the solicitors. His other tasks are subsidiary. In its evidence to the Royal Commission on Legal Services the Barristers' Clerks' Association (BCA), an organisation representing barristers' clerks in negotiations with other bodies, divided the clerk's functions into three groups: the administrative function, the advisory function and the public interest function. In the first group it distinguished forty-two tasks, ranging from negotiating brief fees to reviewing the accommodation of the chambers to taking telephone messages. The second group contained one task, that of advising the barristers on what direction to take at crucial points in their career. In the third group there were six tasks concerned with handling relationships with solicitors, list officers and the BCA's relationship with the Bar.

As the above makes clear, and as the rest of the book will show, the barrister's clerk has a wide range of duties delegated to him. The ostensible rationale of his existence is to relieve the barrister of the day-to-day routines of office administration so that the latter can concentrate entirely on legal work. But, as will be seen later, the clerk does much of the 'dirty work' of the Bar.[13] He fulfils a role that would be difficult, both theoretically and practically, for the Bar to do without. For example, he generates work for barristers, permitting them the claim that they conform to their rule against advertising: he can refuse to accept work on a barrister's behalf by, say, charging an exorbitant fee, allowing barristers to say that they conform to the supposedly inviolate cab-rank rule.[14]

Barristers' clerks are one of the smallest occupational groups in England and Wales, though it is not easy to determine their exact number. One obstacle is the difficulty of defining what constitutes a barrister's clerk. In a typical set of chambers, in addition to the senior clerk, there could be several junior clerks and 'girls' who fill a role half-way between that of typist and clerk. From the *Bar List* (1981) the numbers of senior clerks are easily counted. The result is shown in table 1. And paired clerkships are made as shown in table 2.

Table 1

Senior clerks	London	Provincial	Total
Male	173	74	247
Female	8	25	33
Pairs	26*	12*	38
Total	207	111	318

* This figure represents the number of clerks; the number of clerkships is half the number.
Source. Bar List (1981).

Table 2

Paired clerkships	London	Provincial	Total
Male	9	5	14
Female	1*	0	1
Mixed	3	1	4
Total	13	6	19

* There is, also, one triple female clerkship, not included here.
Source. Bar List (1981).

When Johnstone and Hopson (1967: 426) surveyed clerks they included in their computations junior clerks who performed similar tasks to senior ones. They gave the ratio, then, of juniors to seniors as one and a half to one, which resulted in a total of almost 650 clerks. It might be realistic to adopt, in 1981, ratios of two or three to one, which would result in totals of approximately 600 or 900 clerks. In any case the numbers are small. Benson (1979: I, para. 34.11) commented that the overhead expenses of staffing a barrister's chambers are much lower than those of a solicitor because the ratio of staff to barristers is in the order of one to four, whereas in a solicitor's office the equivalent ratio is one to nearly one and a half (Benson 1979: II, table 16.10).

A further complication has been introduced by the Barristers' Clerks' Association, which wants the definition of clerk to be restricted to those who have had at least five years' experience in clerking. Such a restrictive definition would exclude many junior and some senior clerks who were appointed from outside the normal career channels. The restriction is aimed primarily at this latter group in order to establish a closed shop.

One feature immediately apparent from the tables is that most senior clerks are male and do not share their authority within chambers with other clerks.[15] The percentage of women clerks in the provinces, 22·5 per cent, is much greater than that of London women clerks, at 4 per cent. In London the Bar is more concentrated and has a longer history than the provincial Bar. With the diffuse spread of chambers in the provinces, the opportunities for women to enter are more numerous, for there is a conspicuous lack of trained clerks outside London except in two or three of the larger cities. Paired clerkships are disliked by the majority of clerks: they do not like sharing authority; they view it as damaging to good decision-making. But there has been a slight increase in their numbers since 1976, from eleven to nineteen. The chairman of the BCA claimed that most, if not all, paired clerkships were not partnerships of co-equals but involved degrees of superordination and subordination. However, a paired clerkship is sometimes arranged in order to facilitate the succession of senior clerks in the chambers.

The single most contentious point raised about barristers' clerks by their critics is the form of their remuneration. Clerks generally receive a clerk's fee which is paid by way of a percentage commission. They take great pride in their commissions, though it may, to some, appear a dubious form of payment within the Bar, which considers its own fees *honoraria* and is unable to sue for them. Critics (e.g. Zander, 1968) condemn the clerk's fee for the reason that clerks have a personal stake in extracting the largest possible sum from the client. Superficially the criticism sounds plausible, but it ignores the manner in which clerks conduct their business. Overcharging would simply prevent solicitors from returning to a particular set of chambers. The clerk's goal is to generate a constant supply of work. The fixing of fees thus requires careful deliberation.[16] Of course, there are occasions when they do overcharge.

The clerk's fee has an interesting history. Megarry (1962: 61) attributes its origin to the purchase of candles needed for conferences with clients, which were generally held after the day's proceedings in court. How true this is no one knows. Before 1971 and the decimalisation of the currency, clerks received a separate fee. There were scales which regulated it.[17] For example, in the early 1950s, on the High Court scales, a 100 guinea brief was £100 plus 100s barrister, plus £2.10s clerk—total, £107 10s.[18] These were the clerk's fees allowed on taxation by the court.

In the aftermath of the first world war inflation had severely reduced clerks' earnings, which were still tied to the scales. Some of the scales were raised, but the clerks were not satisfied. In 1919 they floated the idea that barristers earning over £2,000 a year should pay their clerks a shilling out of every guinea earned in addition to the scale fees. The Bar Council did not support the idea, but it eventually caught on. Clerks' fees remained in this form until 1971, when, as part of a rationalisation of counsel's fees, the separate clerk's fee was incorporated into the counsel's fees. The clerk was to receive a percentage, five per cent as of right, and up to another five per cent would be negotiable.[19]

Being a 'ten per cent man' has acquired enormous importance for clerks. For many, to accept less is to lose esteem. To put it another way, one clerk said, 'the barrister earns ninety per cent of the clerk's fee'. The Royal Commission on Legal Services' survey of barristers' clerks' incomes showed that the largest group of respondents (42 per cent) received ten per cent commission and also made a contribution to chambers' expenses.[20]

The Royal Commission found that clerks divided into two main groups: those who received five to seven per cent of gross fees and made no contribution to chambers' expenses, and those who received eight to ten per cent and did make a contribution. A small group, less than ten per cent of the respondents, received a salary alone.

The example of Arthur Magraw, senior clerk to Sir Michael Havers, QC, then Conservative shadow Attorney General, shows clearly some of the difficulties that have arisen over clerks' percentage commissions.[21] The barristers in Magraw's chambers asked him to take a reduction in his commission from ten to eight per cent. He agreed, provided he no longer had to pay the two junior clerks. The barristers refused to accept this condition, and Magraw was dismissed. He claimed unfair dismissal. Part of the problem generally has been caused by the increase in the size of chambers, leading to large increases in clerks' incomes.

Arthur Magraw failed in his claim. The industrial tribunal ruled that he was an independent self-employed contractor, thus he could not claim to have been unfairly dismissed. The contractual position of barristers' clerks has always appeared somewhat mysterious. Their tax position illustrates the complexity of the situation. Simons (1970: 343) discusses two arrangements: either the clerk makes arrangements with each member of chambers, or the head of chambers may make the arrangements with each member for the clerk's contributions to be paid to himself; he will then hand them over to the clerk. The pooling arrangement is not much used now. Under it, a clerk is considered an employee of the head of chambers; under the other system the situation is unclear. For taxation purposes the Inland Revenue deemed the clerk an employee but allowed him substantial expenses as though self-employed. The position is still in a state of flux.[22]

Despite the high status of the Bar as an occupational group, the general conditions under which it works are almost substandard in contemporary terms. In large part this is the result of the Bar's wish to remain within the confines of the Inns of Court, where many of the buildings are old, cramped and unsuitable. Many chambers now put four barristers to a room. But clerks' rooms are frequently more crowded than those of the barristers they serve. Rarely is any thought given to the layout of the clerks' room.[23] This is surprising, for it is the epicentre of the chambers. On entering a set of chambers, it is invariably the first room encountered. It has several functions: communications centre, store room, typing pool and counselling room. But frequently its appearance conveys an impression that it was added as an afterthought.

Some clerks are now having their rooms redesigned to accommodate modern business methods and machines—photocopiers, telex machines and computers.[24] One senior's clerks' room was so precisely planned that when I went to spend some time there I caused considerable confusion because there was no convenient place for me. I was not accounted for in the design. Another moved his clerks' room to another part of the chambers, where he installed a glass partition and was able to observe the movements of all who entered. Both these arrangements resulted from discussions between clerks, barristers and professional design consultants.

But where the barristers have attempted to impose innovation on the clerk it has been resented. In one set of chambers the barristers employed a time-and-motion study team to improve the efficiency of the clerks' room. The senior clerk was already satisfied with the design of his room. The results of the study eventually vindicated him, the only recommendation being the removal of one door. He noted, with satisfaction, that the study had cost £500 and did little but prove him right.

The most important object in the clerks' room is the telephone. The senior clerk and first junior may have as many as four each. Virtually all the clerk's work is conducted by telephone: receiving messages from solicitors, giving instructions to barristers, sorting out court lists. Even the *Methods Manual for Counsel's Clerks,* issued by the Barristers' Clerks' Association, points out:

It is probably not generally realised that to a large extent the administration of justice in this country is dependent upon the telephone. It is the essential means of communication between the Barrister and his headquarters (chambers—the Barrister's Clerk), between the Clerk of Assize, or Clerk of the Peace and other Clerks of the Lists, or Judges' Clerks and their links (the Barrister's Clerk) in London and the provinces, who discuss, collect and disseminate information generally; and between solicitors (who act for the lay client) and Barristers (also through the Barrister's Clerk). A Barrister's Clerk is in fact speaking or listening on the telephone for a large part of every working day. [BCA (1970): 52]

The importance of the telephone can be gauged by the number of pages—eight in all—devoted to the subject in the manual. One clerk summed it up thus: 'The more time you spend on the phone, the more business you get.' However, it must be used correctly, which means answering it as quickly as possible. Generally, a ringing telephone should be answered within three rings. Any later is considered too slow. The importance and impact of the telephone will become increasingly apparent throughout the book.

Another important item is the diary. It is the main source of information about the barristers' movements.[25] And it provides a measure of the level of business activity: it is a complement to the accounts kept by the clerk. The diary rarely, if ever, leaves the clerks' room, and all the diaries of previous years are stored for record purposes.

Clerks' rooms are generally uninspiring; little attention is given to decoration. The functional aspects override all other considerations. There is, however, one exception. In some large chambers the senior clerk has his own room away from the juniors, where he may hang a picture or two. This type of separation emphasises the counselling role of the senior clerk, and leaves the mundane work to the juniors.

The history of barristers' clerks has gone largely unrecorded.[26] Early records of the Inns of Court refer to clerks, but these were usually apprentice lawyers. Prest (1972: 49) notes that in 1455 apprentices often served their masters at meals. Thorne (1959) describes how in the fourteenth century lawyers employed a manciple to look after their house 'to be assured of a bed and a reasonable dinner' (1959: 80). In the discussion following Thorne's lecture one participant suggested that the manciple was the equivalent of the under-treasurer of an Inn, an office of higher esteem than clerk.

The best known reference to a barrister's clerk is Charles Lamb's description of his father, Lovel, clerk to Samuel Salt, KC:

Lovel took care of everything. He was at once his clerk, his good servant, his dresser, his friend, his 'flapper', his guide, stop-watch, auditor, treasurer. He did nothing without consulting Lovel, or failed in any thing without expecting and fearing his admonishing. He put himself almost too much in his hands, had they not been the purest in the world. He resigned his title almost to respect as a master, if L. could ever have forgotten for a moment that he was a servant. [1903: 176]

Fiction continues to provide the main historical portrayals of clerks. R. S. Surtees portrays a different type of clerk from Lovel in *Handley Cross,* namely Bill Bowker, clerk to Mr Twister of Lincoln's Inn in 1854.

Mr Bowker, or Bill Bowker, as he was generally called, was a stout, square-built, ruddy-complexioned, yellow-haired, bustling, middle-aged man, with a great taste for flash clothes and jewellery. On the present occasion, he sported a smart nut-brown coat, with a velvet collar; a sky-blue satin stock, secured by numerous pins and brooches; a double-breasted red tartan waistcoat, well laid back; with brownish drab stockingette pantaloons, and Hessian boots. A great bunch of Mosaic seals dangled from a massive chain of the same material; and a cut steel guard, one passing over his waistcoat, secured a pair of mother-of-pearl-cased eye-glasses, though Bill was not in the least short-sighted.

'You're early,' said Bowker, as Charles [a new pupil] deposited a dripping umbrella in the stand. 'You don't look like a sap either,' added he, eyeing Charles in a free and easy sort of way, for Bill was a real impudent fellow.

'What is the right hour?' inquired Charles, with a schoolboy sort of air.

'Right hour?' exclaimed Bill, 'any time you like—saps come at opening, others at noon, the Honorable not till afternoon. There are two chaps copying precedents now, that the laundress left here at ten last night—(tinkle, tinkle, tinkle, went a little hand-bell). There's the old file himself,' observed Bill, bundling off, adding, as he went, 'be back to you directly.' . . .

The Hon Henry Lollington, the ninth son of an Earl, was quite a used-up West-end man. He was a tall, drawling, dancing sort of a man, in great request at balls, and had a perfect abhorrence of anything coarse or commonplace. He was a mortal enemy to Mr Bowker, whom he kept at arm's length, instead of treating as an equal, as some of the pupils did.

'Mr Bowker,' drawled he, as he encountered that worthy in the passage, 'bring me a piece of paper, and let me give you orders about my letters—I'm going to Bath.'

'Yes, my LUD!' responded Bill, in a loud tone, to let Charles hear what a great man they had among them.

'Dem you, Mr Bowker, I'm not a Lord,' responded the Hon Mr Lollington.

'Beg pardon, my Lud!' replied the imperturbable Bill, bustling out. [1911: 216–17]

Trollope's description of Mr Furnival's clerk, Crabwitz, in *Orley Farm,* written in 1862, characterised Crabwitz's general cynicism. Two extracts illustrate his shrewdly ambivalent attitude towards his principal:

. . . Mr Crabwitz, a gentleman who had now been with Mr Furnival for the last fifteen years, and who considered that no inconsiderable portion of the barrister's success had been attributable to his own energy and genius. Mr Crabwitz was a genteel-looking man, somewhat over forty years of age, very careful as to his gloves, hat, and umbrella, and not a little particular as to his associates. As he was unmarried, fond of ladies' society, and presumed to be a warm man in money matters, he had his social successes, and looked down from a considerable altitude on some men who from their professional rank might have been considered as his superiors. He had a small batchelor's box down at Barnes, and not unfrequently went abroad in the vacations. [1956: 113]

'. . . you're cross [said Mr Furnival] because I've kept you in town a little too long. Come, Crabwitz, you must forget all that. You have worked very hard this year past. Here is a cheque for fifty pounds. Get out of town for a fortnight or so, and amuse yourself.'
'I'm sure I'm very much obliged, sir,' said Crabwitz, putting out his hand and taking the cheque. He felt that his master had got the better of him, and he was still a little melancholy on that account. He would have valued his grievance at that moment almost more than the fifty pounds, especially as by the acceptance of it he surrendered all right to complain for some considerable time to come. [1956: 254]

Has the core of the barrister's clerk's job changed since the nineteenth century? In 1976 a senior clerk described his tasks: 'a barrister's clerk does everything for his governor, even sewing on his fly-buttons, because the typist couldn't do it, as there was no time to take his trousers off.' The remainder of this book explores some of that 'everything'.

NOTES

1 Norman Birkett, quoted in Podium, *Law Society's Gazette,* 27 April 1977: 353.
2 Zander (1968: 83).
3 See Wickenden (1975: 15).
4 For example, see Walker (1980). Note that Benson (1979), in addition to the mainstream legal profession, examined the role of paralegals.
5 Benson (1979: I, table 2.3). However, nobody knows for certain the number of paralegals in England and Wales. But they are probably increasing in number, as in the United States. And barristers' clerks

may be considered a type of paralegal. See Johnstone and Flood (1982); Benson (1979: chs. 31, 34); Brickman (1971); Endacott (1975); Fry (1973); and the forthcoming study of American paralegals by Quintin Johnstone and Martin Weglinsky.

6   But see Foster (1973): solicitors are located primarily in the main shopping areas. And see also Benson (1979: I, paras. 4.28–4.33).

7   There is one exception to this rule, namely the Wellington Street chambers in Covent Garden, London. This set was established with the principle of sharing fees according to need. See their evidence submitted to the Royal Commission on Legal Services.

8   See, however, Boulton (1975: 12–14) and Senate (1980: Annex 14, para. 172). A barrister can accept instructions direct from a lay client where the client is normally outside the United Kingdom and the work is not substantially connected with United Kingdom law.

9   In order to qualify to be called to the Bar, a student must ordinarily eat thirty-six dinners at the hall of his or her Inn. Nowadays eating dinners rarely adds to the student's education, but it is a necessary chore. The origins of this ritual lie in the Middle Ages, when the Inns of Court were responsible for the education of lawyers. See Benson (1979: I, paras. 39.49–55); Warren (1978).

10   Pupilage is a twelve-month unpaid apprenticeship undertaken at the close of the academic and postgraduate vocational training. Any barrister who has continuously practised for five years may take on a pupil. The pupil reads his pupilmaster's papers, follows him to court, and occasionally does some drafting for him. See Hazell (1978a).

11   Boulton (1975: 58) says, 'A barrister must not practise unless he is a member of a professional chambers . . .' and has 'the services of the clerk who is the clerk of the chambers and the use of the chambers' administration and facilities to the extent necessary for the proper conduct of his practice' (note omitted). And further: 'A barrister may not be a member of professional chambers where the wife or husband is the clerk' (1975: 59). See also Senate (1980: para. 26), and Halsbury (1973: para. 1119).

12   My conception of fixer is borrowed from Boissevain's characterisation of a broker (1974: 198); see chapter 4.

13   Cf. Hughes (1971).

14   See Boulton (1975: 6) for the general statement of the rule, and (1975: 32–41) for the exceptions to the rule. See also Senate (1980: paras. 21, 50–62).

15   There are no statistics to indicate how many clerks are members of ethnic minorities or other nationalities.

16   See chapter 4.

17   Abel-Smith and Stevens (1967: 56n) write: 'Originally any payment for the clerk on the barrister's brief fee had been "voluntary and small". Gradually the practice grew up of clerks specifying payments for themselves and ultimately this practice was sanctioned by the judges and accepted by Taxing Officers. As the result of representations by the Law Society, a scale was fixed in 1834. This was increased in 1835. In

1850 there were complaints that clerks were demanding unauthorised fees "with a pertinacity, and often with a rudeness, painful to resist; and, on that account, the claims have been ordinarily submitted to". The Law Society resolved that it was opposed to the principle of barristers' clerks being paid on a percentage basis. Law Society, *Annual Report,* 1850, p. 31. But the system continued.'

18 The evidence of the BCA to the Evershed Committee on Supreme Court Practice and Procedure (see chapter 7) provides the scale of clerks' fees as laid down in the Rules of the Supreme Court, 0. 65, r. 27 (51): the following fees are to be allowed to counsel's clerks:

Upon a fee under five guineas	2s 6d
Five guineas and under ten guineas	5s 0d
Ten guineas and under twenty guineas	10s 0d
Twenty guineas and under thirty guineas	15s 0d
Thirty guineas and under fifty guineas	£1 0s 0d
Fifty guineas and upwards: per cent	£2 10s 0d
On consultations, senior's clerk	5s 0d
On consultations, junior's clerk	2s 6d
On conferences	5s 0d

One guinea = £1 1s 0d = £1·05p.

19 See chapter 7.

20 The consultants of the Royal Commission on Legal Services, Coopers & Lybrand, did not obtain a good response rate to their survey of senior clerks' earnings— only fifty-three per cent. The consultants termed it 'barely adequate' (Benson, 1979: II, s. 14).

21 See 'Barristers: one man and his clerk', *The Economist,* 20 May 1978: 26.

22 See chapter 7.

23 Even the *Methods Manual* (BCA, 1970: 71) devotes only a mere half-page to design under the heading 'General'.

24 See chapter 7, n. 22.

25 A typical diary entry may appear thus:

> *Keep free in morning—meeting of chambers 11 a.m.*
> A.J.
> 2.15 *conference Re: Cyril Simons Smith & Co.*

> *Brighton Crown Ct   Sherman, Sherman (part heard)*
> C.M.
> 4.30 *conf. Re: Hillbank Warehousing v. Jones Pattison*

> *Brighton CC (p.h.)   Sherman, Sherman*
> F.R.
> ~~*Clerkenwell M/C (sect. 2) R v. Regis   WUNLC*~~
> ~~4.30 *conf. Knox v. Knox   WUNLC*~~
> ~~5.30 *conf. Phillips v. Phillips   WUNLC*~~

The initials on the left are those of the barrister, and they are arranged in descending order of call, with the most senior at the top. The name to the far right is that of the instructing solicitor. 'p.h.' means part heard, that is, a trial which is continuing. M/C refers to magistrates' courts. The lines through the last three items indicate cancellations because of the continuing Brighton Crown Court trial.

26 Even the comprehensive Holdsworth's *History of English Law* (1966) has no reference to barristers' or counsel's clerks.

Chapter 2
CAREER PATTERNS AND CONTINGENCIES

The tribe of clerks was an obvious one and here I discerned two remarkable divisions. There were the junior clerks of flash houses—young gentlemen with tight coats, bright boots, well-oiled hair, and supercilious lips. Setting aside a certain dapperness of carriage, which may be termed *deskism* for want of a better word, the manner of these persons seemed to me an exact facsimile of what had been the perfection of *bon ton* about twelve or eighteen months before. They wore the cast-off graces of the gentry;—and this, I believe involves the best definition of the class.

The division of the upper clerks of staunch firms, or of the 'steady old fellows', it was not possible to mistake. These were known by their coats and pantaloons of black or brown, made to sit comfortably, with white cravats and waistcoats, broad solid-looking shoes, and thick hose or gaiters.—They had all slightly bald heads, from which the right ears long used to penholding, had an odd habit of standing off on end. I observed that they always removed or settled their hats with both hands, and wore watches, with short gold chains of a substantial and ancient pattern. Theirs was the affectation of respectability;—if indeed there be an affectation so honourable. [Poe (1978): 508–9]

Outside every set of barristers' chambers is a signboard listing the names of those who practise there. And this list is arranged according to seniority. At the bottom appears the name of the senior clerk. Although the chambers may employ as many as five or six staff, only the senior clerk is accorded recognition to the outside world.

Before the last war the modest size of a set of chambers required a staff of only a senior clerk and a 'boy'. In general 'boys' were exploited. One, possibly apocryphal, story has it that boys used to steal their barristers' wigs and sell them to other barristers as a means of supplementing their meagre income. A boy remained so until he acquired his own chambers as senior clerk; there was no intermediate stage. Nowadays a junior clerk's position has become competitive with that of a senior clerk's in its range of inducements: for example, a junior clerk has guaranteed security and a guaranteed income.

Entrants are recruited at all levels, and advancement depends almost entirely on the clerk's ability to manipulate his network of contacts as well as satisfy his principals. The progression of a typical career is to start as a young boy, graduate to junior clerk and finally become a senior clerk.

In the following sections I will outline the ideal-typical career timetable of a barrister's clerk, and the problems encountered along it.

RECRUITING BARRISTERS' CLERKS

The stereotypes of different occupations frequently encourage or discourage people to enter those occupations. Physiology, for example, is less attractive than medicine because of its dearth of esteemed public stereotypes (Becker and Carper, 1956: 291). A similar picture can be drawn in the legal profession. The title of lawyer, whether barrister or solicitor, elicits some recognition and response, although real knowledge as to what constitutes a lawyer may be absent. The stereotype of the barrister's clerk, however, is virtually non-existent. Many recruits have no idea of what a clerk is or does.

The majority are recruited as boys at school-leaving age. Senior clerks need a boy to do the menial tasks in the chambers. The small number of clerks involved, in addition to their low visibility, removes any element of open competition for vacancies. Normally, recruits enter the occupation sponsored by someone connected with the legal profession.

One junior clerk was introduced into the Temple by his cousin, who was a solicitor's clerk. Another became a clerk through the help of a neighbour. Edgar Bowker offers a typical view of how a young boy may become a clerk.

It was my mother who was responsible for choosing my career . . . Among [her] friends was a daughter of Mr Justice Wills, one of the most famous judges on the Bench of that day. To this daughter my mother confided her desire that, now I had reached a school-leaving age—I was nearly fourteen—she would like me to get a situation in some nice office where there were prospects of 'getting on'.
'I will speak to my father about the boy', said Miss Wills, and, sure enough, one fateful day I was instructed to make my way to Cheyne Court, Chelsea, for the purpose of an interview with the great man.
It was not without some awe and trepidation that I made my call, to find a

kindly-spoken man, who asked me all sorts of questions, and then said he would send me along to a barrister friend who would take me into his office . . .

Behold me then, a boy of not quite fourteen, installed in the chambers at Temple Gardens as an office boy, with Mr Boydell Houghton, at the princely wage of eight shillings a week. [Bowker (1947): 20–1]

The young boy entering the Temple usually has no expectations of a specific career. On the whole most clerks, like Bowker, were influenced to enter the occupation. In some instances a preference for working in 'the law' led to a job in clerking. One young clerk wanted to become a lawyer, especially a barrister, but gave up the idea when he realised it meant going to college. His school careers master guided him into clerking, which required no formal qualifications.

The age of recruits has risen in line with the general increase in school-leaving ages. Before 1945 many entered the Temple at thirteen or fourteen, which had the effect of extending the length of time a boy spent as general dogsbody in the chambers. Today that period is much shorter.

Initial recruitment sometimes occurs at more senior levels—such as first junior or senior clerk. However, in an occupation where tradition and experience are highly valued this type of lateral recruitment arouses hostility and resentment. For example, when a solicitor's clerk was employed as a senior, news of the chambers' collapse a year later was welcomed by those in the Temple who blamed it on the outsider's incompetence. But recruitment as a first junior clerk is received more favourably; and a newcomer may do a short stint as 'dogsbody' in order to become acquainted with his new environment and at least appear to be going through the proper rites of passage.

Choosing a new recruit is a haphazard business for the senior clerk. At best he puts his trust in the recommendation of the boy's sponsor, if he has one, otherwise the only other guide is an interview with a short probation following. But, as one clerk said, 'How can you find out what a person is like in an interview? It's really a case of trial and error.' The senior clerk looks for a tidy appearance, quick wits and some intelligence. At one interview a boy who was well dressed and eager, but nervous, was quizzed about clerks and the law. The boy knew little but felt he wanted to work in the law. The senior clerk described the range of tasks and the way in which the youth could expect to progress in his career. 'It'll take you about four or five years to learn the job, and as you make contacts and become experienced you'll go up to first junior clerk and then senior clerk on commission. The harder you work the more you'll get.' In particular the clerk was concerned whether the youngster would stay in his chambers which, as a Chancery set, 'is a lot different to crime, a lot *duller*'. Another applicant, untidy in appearance, declined an offer to visit the Law Courts and spend some time in the chambers because he had to pack for his holiday. The clerk read this as a sign of indifference to the job and so hired the first comer.

Different criteria are applied when clerks are hired at a more senior level. 'Outsider' senior clerks need to have some managerial and administrative skills. Outsiders are usually employed by new sets of chambers, which are unable to attract conventional senior clerks.[1] For example, a group of pupils nearing the end of their pupilages and unable to find tenancies elected to set up their own chambers—a risky venture. They invited a young solicitor's clerk to work for them. Another set stipulated that the clerk's political sympathies be the same as theirs. Ethnic chambers tend to select clerks from the same ethnic groups. For black sets of chambers the choice of an outsider is a necessity because there are so few trained black clerks.

Under the rubric of minorities may be included, in addition to ethnic minorities, women. Most clerks are white British males and the standard role for women has been that of laundress or cleaner. However, since 1945 their status has improved. Women are generally viewed as suitable for menial tasks like typing and carrying messages, but they are sometimes promoted to the level of first junior clerk. Very few have ever become senior clerks. The prevalent feeling is that women do not fit in the 'smoking room' atmosphere of the Temple; the view is even held that they are less intelligent and capable than men. A member of the BCA said, 'Although we do not object to women, they are difficult to place.' But among the younger, more politically motivated members of the Bar the view is gaining force that women may actually make better clerks because they are less bound by tradition and conservatism.

Essentially the sets of chambers outside the conventional field have the least to offer a 'formally' trained clerk, and therefore have to employ outsiders. The result is a paradoxical situation where pressure from clerks in general—especially the Barristers' Clerks' Association—is to recruit from within their ranks, yet few clerks are attracted to such risky posts. The Senate of the Inns of Court has recognised the problem but as yet has proposed no solution.[2]

The Barristers' Clerks' Association has attempted to repair some of the defects of the recruitment process, but with scant success. The first indication of interest on its part occurred in 1962 when the chairman was asked to prepare a memorandum for the Central Youth Employment Executive.[3] Later the BCA opened a register of vacancies, some of which are advertised in the Court List Publication Room at the Law Courts.[4]

In conjunction with the Inner London Education Authority the chairman of the BCA holds, each year, an 'open day' for twelve to fifteen schools' careers masters to help acquaint them with the clerk's job and environment. However, the existence of the one school leaving point during the year produces an uneven supply of potential recruits when vacancies arise throughout the year.

The net impact of the BCA's recruitment activities has been small. Instead, clerks rely on their network of contacts. Rejected candidates are referred to the BCA secretary for possible inclusion in his list.

The remaining source of entry is nepotism. But it is not as widespread as might be thought. The instances I encountered numbered fewer than a handful. Nevertheless father-to-son succession does confer a degree of stability and continuity. Very occasionally succession has been known to run for three or four generations in the same chambers. In one set the clerk took over from his uncle. In another, virtually the entire staff was from the same family.

Conversely some clerks took positive action to prevent their sons (no one ever spoke of daughters) from becoming clerks. They had a distinct wish to better their children's lot. For example, one clerk wanted his son to become a solicitor, because 'He'll make more money that way—much more than me.' The main deterrent is education. Putting a child through university not only raises expectations but effectively raises a barrier to clerking.

Stage one: the boy. Novicehood is the most daunting period in a clerk's career. The young man is thrust into an archaic, hierarchically structured society which, at first, only confounds him. A boy's duties are the least stimulating: he carries the barristers' books and robes to court, he takes messages round the Temple, he makes the tea and fetches the sandwiches for lunch. A familiar morning sight in the Temple (and the other Inns) is that of boys rushing to the Law

Courts with bundles of law reports in their arms or on small trolleys.
One clerk vividly recalled having to carry about eighty law reports
and legal textbooks to the Royal Courts of Justice—a regular duty he
loathed. Eric Cooper, a clerk, wrote once:

I remember well myself, when I first came into the Temple as a boy in the
chambers of the Hon. Victor Russell. The Hon. Victor Russell always had
tea brought to him every day at 4 o'clock, and I was the boy and I used to
make the tea. His tea was China tea, and he had it in a green teapot, and he
had a green plate on which he had digestive biscuits (two in number), and he
wanted this at 4 o'clock precisely. If I was late there was trouble. The Earl of
Drogheda liked his tea as near to 4 o'clock as possible, but, of course, it could
not actually be at 4, it was probably two or three minutes past, and he had a
blue teapot, and a blue cup, and a blue plate, and one chocolate digestive
biscuit, and he had Indian tea. [Cooper (n.d.): 3]

A boy may have to survive such work for up to eighteen months to
two years before he is promoted.

The senior clerk usually adopts a paternal attitude. One clerk
described how his first senior disapproved of his wearing a suit: it
was above his station. Instead he would have to wear a jacket and
flannels. Being poor, he could not afford a jacket, so the senior clerk
gave him the money. In fact the senior clerk virtually acted as
surrogate father.

All the clerks I talked to emphasised the importance of the training
they received from their first senior clerk. From him they learned the
foundations of their future clerking styles; whether, for example, to
be dictatorial or manipulative in their dealings with barristers.[5]
From him they came to recognise and make sense of the complex and
paradoxical status relations that exist in the legal profession. On the
one hand the boy realises that barristers (apart from judges) hold the
position of greatest prestige and status. Yet he sees the senior clerk
exercise considerable influence over barristers. Furthermore the
solicitor, despite his 'inferior' status, is seen to be the one who
provides the business. It was best epitomised by one clerk who was
told by his first senior, 'You are low in the hierarchy here, but'
(pointing at a pupil barrister) *'he is lower than you.'*

There is little formal in-job training. Boys learn by observing
what goes on around them. What instruction there is is most
frequently given by the first junior. For example, the boy learns
about fees for different cases by typing fee notes and keeping the
ledgers up to date, then having his work reviewed by the junior.

At this point in his career he is at his most expendable unless he proves his worth. If he is thought slow or dull-witted he is rejected, effectively, from any clerking job. A senior clerk explained his sacking of a boy:

He had to go; he was hopeless, completely thick. He couldn't even remember the governors' phone numbers in chambers. He used to give the wrong dates to the list office; never kept our lists up to date. I gave him a few weeks to find another job. He's working in a warehouse now.

In surviving the 'donkey work' the young clerk is ready to search for a more responsible junior post. Vertical promotion in the same set, from boy to senior clerk, is rare. To advance, he must move to another set. Several clerks mentioned their reluctance to leave their first set of chambers. They moved only because the senior clerk told them to.

Stage two: the junior clerk. When a boy begins to advance, his critical faculties should be sufficiently developed for him to appraise the reputation of various sets of chambers. Of course, his senior will advise him; he may even suggest that the young clerk change from one type of chambers to another—e.g. from criminal to commercial law—as a means of broadening his experience.[6] Indeed, the choice of chambers is crucial, because his peers will judge him, in part, on the standing of those chambers. One young clerk who had moved from boy in successful civil law chambers to first junior in prosecution chambers told me he was happy with his new post. But others felt he had taken the job without enough experience elsewhere. The new post had two handicaps. It did not 'stretch' him enough, and it tended to keep him out of contact with other clerks. The pressure to generate work for counsel is missing in prosecution chambers, because the briefs are sent direct from the Director of Public Prosecutions: this young clerk was not forced to socialise.

During this period the junior clerk's responsibilities increase steadily, in some cases to the point where he will actually be fulfilling the role of the senior clerk. For example, it is normal for the clerk to the Attorney General to devote his whole working time to his principal's business[7] while still remaining senior clerk to his chambers. Here, the junior clerk, in effect, takes over the running of the chambers. Senior and junior clerks frequently divide the work between themselves according to its 'outdoor' and 'indoor' content: the division of labour is decided by the senior clerk. 'Indoor' work entails dealing with clients over the telephone and maintaining the diary. 'Outdoor' work includes making and maintaining business and business-related connections, such as entertaining other clerks, solicitors' clerks, solicitors and confidential chats with the 'governors'. Sometimes the idea of 'outdoor' work is abused. In his autobiography Aylett (1978: 36–7) tells how his second senior clerk would slip off to the pub for most of the day, leaving him to do all the work. Nevertheless, maintaining an expanding network of contacts is of supreme importance. One clerk criticised his junior for failing in this. 'One point about [Andrew] is that he doesn't know anybody in the Temple. I keep telling him to make friends, even if he only sees them once a month. He should get himself known—you *have* to in order to get on.' As Hall (1948) has noted, in order to get on in any occupation it is necessary to be sponsored before one is accepted by its 'inner fraternity'.

To a limited extent the training of junior clerks was institutionalised in 1971 with the start of a series of lectures and, in 1972, the introduction of a written examination.[8] The lectures are based on the *Methods Manual for Counsel's Clerks* (1970)—which is completely out of date—the *Conduct and Etiquette at the Bar* (Boulton, 1975) and the experience of the lecturers. The course covers court procedure, book-keeping, chambers administration and the etiquette of the Bar. But the training scheme is entirely voluntary. The Barristers' Clerks' Association reports show that an average of fifteen juniors have been participating in the scheme each year. In an effort to upgrade it the BCA is farming out the lectures to a local further education college, and introducing minimum qualifications—three Ordinary level GCE passes—as a prerequisite for taking the course. Junior clerks who fail to meet the preliminary standards take a different course to raise them to the required level. Despite the efforts of the BCA, the scheme is unlikely to succeed gloriously. Practical experience is still seen as the paramount qualification. Even the president of the BCA (a proponent of the training scheme) extolled the virtues of experience in his inaugural lecture:

Those who survived and found themselves selected as senior clerks had had the additional advantage of being thrown into daily constant contact with members of the Bar, men and women of erudition and ability whose professional conduct is at the highest possible level. What better University could a barrister's clerk have or desire? [Newland (1971): 2]

The period spent as junior clerk has, since the late 1900s, lengthened considerably. And attitudes towards payment have also changed. I mentioned earlier the exploitation of juniors by their senior clerks. With the lengthening of the juniors' working life the Bar Council and the BCA decided an effort should be made to increase their incomes. According to the chairman of the BCA, this has resulted in fewer junior clerks applying for senior clerkships because the increased responsibilities may outweigh any rise in earnings: the incentive has diminished. Thus one clerk expected to remain a first junior for ten years before looking for his own chambers.

A first junior in a successful chambers generally receives a commission of one or two per cent of the gross fees in addition to his salary.[9] Fringe benefits may also be provided. One junior had a telephone installed in his house, paid for by the chambers; another was lent money by his senior to buy a house when he married. Most senior clerks favoured higher salaries for their juniors; but some baulked at the idea of introducing commissions, because, as one argued, junior clerks 'begin to think they can do a senior clerk's job after a couple of years' experience. *Nonsense*. They need more.'

The main cause of the junior clerk's longer working life has been a slowing down in the growth of numbers of sets of chambers. Conversely, the size of chambers has grown dramatically,[10] and the internal structure has developed bureaucratic tendencies. Thus the clerk's job, in its intermediate stage—junior clerk—offers greater security than when chambers' comprised only a few members. But most junior clerks expect to have their own chambers by the time they are thirty or thereabouts.

The decision to become a senior is not easy. First, the clerk must find chambers worth clerking for. Vacancies in the high-prestige chambers are strongly competed for. Second, he must calculate the cost of assuming a senior clerkship against the probable future returns. If the chambers are profitable his earnings will be considerably higher than as a junior.[11] Ideally a junior would prefer to take on a well balanced chambers rather than a set with 'too much tail' (too many inexperienced counsel). Third, he must steel himself to be the final decision-maker and accept ultimate responsibility. As one senior clerk put it, 'When you're senior clerk, then the buck stops here. I can't pass it on to anyone now, that's my junior's prerogative.'

Stage three: the senior clerk. If a junior clerk is fortunate enough to take over an established set of chambers his life will be relatively unproblematic. If, however, he joins a less successful set, then he will have to develop his keenest entrepreneurial and managerial skills. Clerking a new set, for example, requires that he invest not only his time and energy but his own money. He has to persuade solicitors and barristers' clerks to give his chambers as much surplus work as they can, until they can attract sufficient regular work.

One fundamental principle always obtains when a new senior begins his term: no clerk believes his predecessor was doing his job properly. Several took pride in showing me the improvements in the chambers' diaries when they took over. For example, in one set the diaries showed the three most senior barristers supplementing their Crown Court defence work with cases at magistrates' courts. But there were still long gaps between. A year later the pages were filling up with Crown Court work and the senior members were discarding the magistrates' court work. Within three years the clerk had reached the point where he was beginning to have a surplus of cases. It is difficult, however, to separate the effect of the clerk from the general rise in the amount of legal work in the past few years. Of course most clerks claim that barristers owe their success to them. In some instances the contribution can be identified, as in the case of a clerk who moved to a criminal prosecution chambers and decided to bring in criminal defence work—something never considered previously.

For clerking a set of chambers, all clerks (with only one or two exceptions) receive a percentage commission of five to ten per cent of their principals' gross fees. But when taking on a new set with, perhaps, only a few junior barristers, the clerk will negotiate a guaranteed minimum income until the level of fees rises sufficiently to afford him a commission. Occasionally barristers have viewed a guaranteed income as a kind of long-term loan repayable by a subsequent reduction in the commission. As a counter-measure some clerks to new chambers are forgoing a minimum income and electing to take a percentage from the start. This makes the junior stage more important, because the junior will have to save a portion of his income to carry him through the initial period as senior clerk.

Clerks have taken other precautionary measures against possible commission reductions. The main one is for the senior to contribute to chambers' expenses, mainly by paying the salary of one or two members of the staff. For example, one senior clerk maintained that he was the second largest contributor to expenses after the head of chambers. It is not always a foolproof method, however, as several clerks have been forced to take reductions despite the contributions they have made. Some have resigned rather than accept the ignominy of a reduction; they strongly believe in being 'a ten per cent man'. [12]

Apart from losing part of his commission, the other main contingency a senior clerk faces is the loss of some of his barristers. If a set of chambers fragments owing to, say, personality differences among the members a senior effectively has two choices. Either he can revert to junior status in a different set, something not often done, or he can join one of the segments. One clerk had two such schisms occur. On the first occasion he aligned himself with the break-away faction, which involved him in a search for new chambers. The second time he lost five out of thirty barristers, and his junior went too.

These splits usually occur when a middle-range barrister (of, say, ten years' call) rebels against the authority of the head of chambers and wants to establish his own, taking like-minded colleagues with him. An astute clerk must be constantly aware of the shifts in mood of his barristers, and any possible emotional confrontations. His job is to monitor drifts towards disequilibrium and draw them back into equilibrium if necessary and if possible.

Other losses occur as a result of official and judicial appointments. And they can have a dramatic effect on the clerk's profit margin. Most of these appointments are from among Queen's Counsel, who are not only profitable but also, in many instances, are the mainstay of the chambers' reputation. The following example is extreme, but it shows in a magnified way the effects of such losses. A clerk in his late twenties was promoted to senior in a very successful specialist chambers which was, however, quite small, with only nine members. In the space of a few years he lost his three most senior counsel—all silks—to the Bench. They were appointed prematurely over the heads of several other eminent QCs in that specialist bar. At the age of thirty-three the clerk was left with no silks, too much tail and a smaller income than when he started. The danger is exacerbated when there is only one QC in the chambers. A replacement should always be ready to fill the vacant slot.

One further contingency is likely to arise more often in the future.

In recent years some chambers have opened annexes in the provinces. They are nominally headed by the London head of chambers, although in fact they constitute a separate entity. The clerk in London is also clerk to the annexe, and spends some time actually working for it, but a junior is usually installed to manage the day-to-day affairs. The perceived benefits are that local counsel are provided for the solicitors in the district; that the London counsel have a base they can use for local conferences;[13] and that the annexe is an outlet and training ground for old pupils of the London chambers. The drawback is that, in time, the annexe may become self-sufficient and hive off from the London chambers. As one clerk put it, 'Annexes are double-edged swords.'[14]

If a senior clerk does his job well he may find himself on a plateau, with little to do but administrate. As the reputation of the chambers grows and becomes self-fulfilling, his entrepreneurial role diminishes. In time he may come to feel stale. Some retire at this point to start a new career; like the one who became landlord of a pub.

Most do not retire until the end of their working life, however.[15] If a clerk does not want to break abruptly from the environment in which he has spent many years he has the option of becoming a judge's clerk. In the past, when a clerk served only a few barristers, it was common for a senior principal, on appointment to the Bench, to take his clerk with him. Bowker (1947: 292) provides us with a picture of such a scene:

> So when [Norman Birkett] broke the news [that he had been asked to become a judge] to me, and in a rather wistful voice remarked: 'I am afraid this will mean the parting of our ways, Edgar', it was a very sad moment.
> Up till then I had had the good fortune to be closely associated with him for twenty-one years. I had watched him grow up at the Bar, and seen him leap from success to success until he reached the very zenith of his popularity as an advocate. And throughout that time he had always shown me the greatest possible kindness and consideration. In that moment I knew full well that there could never be any thought of leaving Norman Birkett, and I recall the look of pleasure in his eyes when I said: 'I'd like to stay with you, sir.'

Today the relationship between clerk and counsel is not so close; and the financial disincentive in becoming a judge's clerk is considerable.[16] Moreover in 1954 the Supreme Court Officers (Pensions) Act removed the judges' power to bring their clerks with them on appointment to the Bench.[17] The main attraction of a judge's clerkship is its secure retirement pension. A fifty-year-old clerk 'went on the corridor' (as the move is known) because he wanted to manage one person instead of twenty. The composition of his chambers had changed—the older members had retired, so diminishing the loyalty he felt. And he needed only ten years' service to be eligible for pension. The drop in income was outweighed by the greater job security, the pension and the lack of pressure and stress.

Despite their contempt for the civil service,[18] several clerks expressed a desire eventually to become a judge's clerk as a way of tapering off their career. The work is not difficult; it involves planning the judge's diary and other secretarial duties, making the arrangements and accompanying him on circuit.[19]

CONCLUSION

The ideal career follows the pattern of boy, junior clerk and ultimately senior clerk. The first stage is important because it is then that a potential clerk is accepted into the occupation or rejected. Those who are not prepared to wait are soon deterred by the 'dogsbody' work they have to do: they can be 'cooled out' with little regard for their feelings. The ones that remain are subject to the kind of career mechanisms described by Becker and Carper (1956): investment, development of interest and acquisition of skill, acquisition of ideology, internalisation of motives, and sponsorship by the 'inner fraternity' of the occupation. These mechanisms continue to operate until a clerk has become part of the inner fraternity himself.

A young clerk has to invest considerable time in the initial stages of his career. At the beginning, clerking is not attractive; it is confusing and the novice must persevere if he is to make sense of this world. As his understanding grows, the problems of manpower planning and fee-fixing come to represent the real world to him. He practices the skills of scheduling cases, agreeing fees with solicitors and selling barristers for particular cases.

The most important mechanism in Becker and Carper's list is the acquisition of an ideology. The clerk's ideology is received from the senior clerk; he is the arbiter where ethical and moral problems are concerned. The young clerk becomes conversant with the complex relations within the legal profession and how much weight to attach to different allegiances. He enters a 'social world [which] is an orderly arena which serves as a stage on which each participant can carve out of a career. There are special norms of conduct, a set of values, a prestige ladder, and a common outlook toward life— a *Weltanschauung*' (Shibutani, 1962: 136–7). However, with different allegiances pulling him in different directions, he must always put his senior first. For example, when a young junior clerk was ordered to buy some whisky for a barrister under doctor's orders not to drink, he reported the matter to his senior immediately rather than obey the barrister.

A barrister's clerk cannot progress only by identifying with and looking inward to his occupational group. Success depends almost as much on the development of external contacts. He must cultivate solicitors and court officials. It is among these people that he develops and practises his brokerage skills; he 'bridges gaps in communication between persons . . .' (Boissevain, 1974: 148). Frequently clerks are required to balance the conflicting interests of four or five parties in a case. A reputation for unravelling conflicts is therefore essential.

The timing of a clerk's career has altered radically since the 1960s, when the Bar underwent considerable expansion. The boy stage has been compressed, but the time spent as junior clerk has lengthened. And, in effect, junior clerks are compensated for their reduced opportunity of finding a senior clerkship. One effect of opening up the role of the junior has been to lessen the importance of building a set of chambers up. Some juniors now prefer to wait for their own senior clerk to retire and then take his post. Those who take the risk of a new set must face a range of contingencies, some of which could finish their career. In many respects, then, a clerk's career is parallel to that of a barrister, the difference being that the barrister possesses skills which, in the case of failure, are marketable outside the Bar; the clerk's skills are not so easily transferable.

NOTES

1 For example, see the evidence submitted to the Royal Commission on Legal Services by the Wellington Street chambers.
2 In its evidence to Benson the Senate of the Inns of Court said, 'New sets of chambers being formed, when composed mainly of young barristers, present a problem. The uncertainty of success, and the low earnings at the beginning result in few applicants from the more senior first juniors. Those appointed have accordingly in some cases, been less

experienced than the Senate would wish to see, especially as the start of a new set requires particular skills from the clerk.' (Section III, A.22.2.)

3 See BCA Annual Report, 1962.

4 Some chambers are now advertising outside the normal confines of the Bar. The following advertisement appeared in Professional & Executive Recruitment's journal, *Executive Post,* 13 November 1981:

BARRISTERS CLERK

Negotiable Remuneration   London EC4

This is an excellent opportunity for candidates from a variety of backgrounds to consider a post in which negotiating expertise, a flair for public relations and good telephone manner play a vital role. The principals are seeking somebody to deal with solicitors and court staff, receiving cases and negotiating appropriate fees for the barristers services.

You will be keeping records of cases handled, and most importantly, will be expected to 'sell' the principals' professional skills to advantage in the context of legal competence on paper and in court.

Job duties will also include running a small office, so literacy and numeracy are essential, and typing ability would be an asset.

Age is not important as a background in which the above outlined skills have contributed to success. Experience in law, property, sales and other professional spheres, or an ex-service background are just some of the areas the client is willing to consider. Starting salary is negotiable for the initial training period, after which you will have the opportunity to earn commission.

Success in this post can lead to high earnings and remuneration will be discussed at interview stage.

5 See chapter 3.

6 Cf. the civil service promotion procedure, which is regarded as an internal matter, outside the ambit of the Minister (Kellner and Crowther-Hunt, 1980). It is the same with barristers' clerks; barristers have little influence on their careers.

7 The Attorney General does not lose his connection with private practice when in office. See Edwards (1964).

8 See appendix 3.

9 The following tables are taken from a survey of barristers' clerks' earnings prepared for the Royal Commission on Legal Services (Benson, 1979: II, s. 14). The survey did, however, suffer from a poor response rate.

[14.18] Average payments to junior clerks, 1975—76

	£	%
By chambers	1,632	65
By members of chambers	309	12
By senior clerk	586	23
	2,527	100

[14.21] Range of earnings of junior clerks, by age, 1975–76 (£)

Age group	Lower quartile	Median	Upper quartile
Under 19	1,092	1,300	1,500
19–21	1,560	2,000	2,575
22–30	2,500	3,500	4,116
Over 30	2,600	4,185	6,195
All junior clerks	1,456	2,100	3,500

[14.20] Distribution of earnings of junior clerks by age, 1975–76

Age group	All junior clerks No.	%	Percentage of junior clerks Under £2,000	£2,000–£3,999	£4,000–£5,999	£6,000 or above
Under 19	54	100	94	6	–	–
19–21	33	100	45	55	–	–
22–30	64	100	8	55	36	1
Over 30	21	100	14	33	29	24
All junior clerks	172	100	43	37	17	3

10 See chapter 3, note 6.
11 The following tables are from the barristers' clerks' earnings survey:

[14.9] Average gross and net income of senior clerks; 1975–76 (£)

Gross income:	
From chambers	11,537
From other sources	86
	11,623
Less Expenses:	
Junior clerks and other staff	951
Chambers expenses and sundry	390
	1,341
Net income	10,282

[14.10] Range of net income of senior clerks, 1975–76

	£	Ratio to median
Upper quartile	12,850	1.32
Median	9,770	1.00
Lower quartile	6,100	0.62
Average	10,282	1.05

[14.11] Range of net income and average net income of senior clerks by age, 1975–76

Age group	Average net income £	Total No.	%	Percentage of senior clerks*					
				Under £4,000	£4000–£6,999	£7,000–£9,999	£10,000–£12,999	£13,000–£14,999	£15,000 or over
25 or less	4,030	6	100	83	–	–	–	–	–
26–30	7,584	20	100	–	45	35	–	–	–
31–40	11,334	33	100	–	18	30	24	–	24
41–50	12,142	27	100	–	–	22	30	15	26
51–60	11,502	23	100	–	–	22	30	–	26
61–65	7,687	7	100	–	43	–	–	–	–
Over 65	9,186	3	100	–	–	–	–	–	–
All ages	£10,282	119	100	9	17	25	25	6	18

* Percentages have been omitted where there are only one or two clerks in a category.

[14.12] Range of net income of senior clerks by seniority, 1975–76

Years as senior clerk	Total No.	%	Percentage of senior clerks*					
			Under £4,000	£4,000–£6,999	£7,000–£9,999	£10,000–£12,999	£13,000–£14,999	£15,000 or over
1–5	40	100	20	40	20	10	–	10
6–10	27	100	–	–	30	33	–	22
11–20	33	100	–	9	27	27	9	24
21–30	15	100	–	–	27	33	–	20
Over 30	4	100	–	–	–	–	–	–
All senior clerks	119	100	9	17	25	25	6	18

* Percentages have been omitted where there are only one or two clerks in a category.

Barristers' clerks

[14.13] Range of net income of senior clerks by number of principals; 1975–76

No. of principals	No. of senior clerks		Net incomes of senior clerks in 1975–76 (£)		
	No.	%	Lower quartile	Median	Upper quartile
1–5	4	4	–	–	–
6–10	23	19	3,475	4,527	10,022
11–15	41	43	7,133	8,918	11,906
16–20	40	34	9,295	11,527	13,353
Over 20	11	9	–	16,250	–
All senior clerks	119	100	6,100	9,770	12,850

One particular feature of the reported net incomes was the wide range of net incomes of senior clerks, as shown in table 14.10.

12 See *The Economist*, 20 May 1978: 26. Arthur Magraw, senior clerk of Sir Michael Havers QC's chambers, refused to accept a reduction from ten to eight per cent if it meant he had to continue paying his juniors. He was dismissed. He brought an action for unfair dismissal, but the industrial tribunal ruled that he was an independent, self-employed contractor, not an employee; therefore he could not have been wrongfully dismissed. And see the following table.

[14.14] Average gross and net income of senior clerks by method of remuneration, 1975–76

Method of remuneration	Senior clerks		Gross income	Expenses	Net income	Net income as % of gross income
	No.	%	(£)	(£)	(£)	(£)
5% of receipts	19	16	8,936	517	8,419	94
6% or 7% of receipts	21	18	9,685	220	9,465	98
8% or 9% of receipts	22	18	12,349	1,221	11,128	90
10% of receipts	48	40	13,747	2,254	11,493	84
Salary or combination of salary and % of receipts	9	8	8,719	1,115	7,604	87
Total	119	100	11,623	1,341	10,282	88

13 It is a convention that the solicitor always visits the barrister's chambers for conferences with counsel (Boulton, 1975: 15–16).

14 Similar, in some ways, is the situation where a clerk in London works for Queen's Counsel who are based in the provinces. Until 1967 it was normal practice for a provincial barrister, on taking silk, to join a London set of chambers even though he intended to remain elsewhere. The rationale was that the available stock of silks should not be depleted or be difficult to contact because some were based outside London. This practice is no longer enforced (see Boulton, 1975: 60). But some clerks still have provincial silks and are frightened that they will leave in the near future.

15 They may continue in part-time work as consultants to the chambers.

16 According to the Civil Service Commission the salary scale for judges' clerks is £3,829 to £5,165.

17 See chapter 7 for a discussion of the history and impact of the 1954 Act.

18 See chapter 5.

19 Each judge's clerk is issued with two handbooks covering the duties of the clerk and containing essential information such as the correct robes for ceremonial occasions, addresses of judges' lodgings and names of butlers and cooks. One handbook refers to London, the other to the circuits. Clerks of Chancery judges and Appeal Court judges do not travel outside London, as their judges do not go on circuit.

Chapter 3

THE CLERK AND HIS BARRISTER

In this chapter I try to draw out the essential features of the relationship between clerk and barrister. In order to convey the subtle nuances of, and interplay between, the characters I have employed the metaphor of the theatre.[1] This schema is particularly suitable for describing lawyers, especially the Bar, because the theatrical analogies are clearly observable in the courts and the law.[2]

The chapter is in two main parts: the first examines existing analyses of the clerk–barrister relationship; in the second the empirical data are presented and discussed.

FORMAL CONCEPTIONS

Boulton's *Conduct and Etiquette at the Bar* (1975), as a starting point for the formal view, scarcely considers the bonds linking the barrister and his clerk. They are mentioned only occasionally, as, for example, in the rule on negotiating fees:

Brief fees are fixed by arrangement between the instructing solicitor or his clerk, and counsel's clerk, but it is permissible in cases of special difficulty for counsel to discuss the amount of a fee personally with the instructing solicitor. [1975: 52]

Boulton divulges little else on the subject.

Other conceptions are found in the writings of members of the Bar and in the literature distributed by the clerks themselves. First, Megarry (1962: 55):

[The clerk] makes an important contribution to the efficient practice of the law and so to the interests of the public . . . [He] is a complicated cross between a theatrical agent, a business manager, an accountant and a trainer.

This is a more rounded description but, as with the remainder of his Hamlyn lecture, Megarry is attempting to persuade the reader of the purity and excellence of the English lawyer.[3] Desmond Ackner, then chairman of the Bar, put forward the view, in reply to Zander (1968), that:

> The statement that the clerk controls the flow of work in chambers and its distribution to the different barristers working there is, for the most part, false . . . In regard to the point that barristers' clerks are not bound by any ethical or disciplinary code, it should be pointed out that a barrister is always responsible for the conduct of his clerk.[4]

Ackner is endeavouring to show, like Bagehot with the constitution, the 'dignified' side of the professional relationship as opposed to the 'efficient'. His view also reveals his ignorance about barristers' clerks and their ethical concerns.[5] A later writer, Grayson, applauded the barrister's clerk, as 'essential and as permanent to the practice of the law in England and Wales as the right for each party to be heard in the concept of natural justice, as also, too, is his service to the community'.[6] He depicted the clerk as '. . . team manager, secretary, trainer, wet nurse for the fledgeling, father-confessor, accountant, VAT collector for HM Customs and Excise, and also trustee and guardian of each barrister's professional integrity and conduct within his surveillance, all rolled into one'. Again, Grayson is reiterating the complacency of the Bar, omitting any suggestion of conflict. The Royal Commission on Legal Services induced the Bar to think seriously and systematically about clerk–barrister relations. Yet the result, not unexpectedly perhaps, was uncritical:

> [The senior clerk] represents the chambers as a whole—and each barrister individually—in dealings with solicitor clients; by the service he provides and as a PR man for his chambers a good clerk will build up the goodwill of the chambers in all manner of ways extending far beyond merely the efficient promotion of his principal's professional services.
>
> In the case of small work which may be unnamed (i.e. sent to chambers, but not to a particular barrister), he allocates it within chambers. This requires detachment and judgment as well as knowledge of the strengths and weaknesses of the individual barristers he clerks and of the needs of the client concerned.
>
> He advises individual members of chambers throughout their career, for instance as to when it is wise and appropriate to take on heavier work or to take silk, and he brings on his principals whenever he has options open to him. In some cases he is asked by a principal to help him with his personal affairs.[7]

These, then, are the formal or dignified conceptions of the relationship from the standpoint of the Bar. Naturally they reflect the ideology of the Bar and its desire to present a unified front to outside observers. The clerks have done the same. The secretary of the Barristers' Clerks' Association stated in a lecture:

The first real picture of the barrister's clerk is . . . a devoted servant, always watching his Principal's interests and probably being devoted because of the fact that above all he was being employed in a genteel occupation in an important and special profession, the Law, and the work which he used to do in addition to his clerical work, still to some extent today, the barrister's clerk does. [Cooper (n.d.): 8]

And a recruitment brochure issued by the BCA noted:

[The clerk] sees that his barristers are in the right court at the right time, that they are dressed correctly on ceremonial occasions, and informs the family of a barrister of the latter's sudden departure or return from cases in the provinces and elsewhere. He can nurse young barristers of ability along the road to success; established barristers can be at a great loss without him.

The BCA appears concerned to project a subordinate role for the clerk *vis-à-vis* the barrister, yet it is aware of the humble status of some barristers starting practice:

Today, I would guess that virtually no barrister has sufficient means without his practice to survive, . . . It means also that the barristers of today sometimes come, basically, from the same beginnings as the barrister's clerk, whereas all those years ago we came from totally different beginnings. [Cooper (n.d.): 14]

. Finally, the president of the BCA (Newland, 1971) compared Charles Lamb's (1903) description of the relationship between Mr Salt, KC, and his clerk (Lamb's father) with the modern situation and found they were co-extensive:

'He was at once his clerk.' That means that every person who wanted Mr Salt, KC's, assistance had to go to a solicitor who would then go to John Lamb, the clerk, and the latter would then agree what fee Mr Salt, KC, was to be paid and arrange for him to appear in court or settle a will or write an opinion, or whatever the business was. He would then collect and bank the fee.

'His good servant.' Still today many barristers regard their clerk as their servant and if you get called on to do some menial task, do it with a good heart as it is part of the tradition.

'His dresser.' You see that every day in every robing room and you take care to see he has a good supply of clean collars and bands. Dressing your men who are Queen's Counsel for the Lord Chancellor's breakfast and for court levees requires expert knowledge.

'His friend.' Well, the relationship between a barrister and his clerk often is most remarkable. Thrown together so constantly as they are, a bond grows up between them that is difficult to describe—it has to be experienced.

'His flapper.' That has beaten most people. It must refer to the fact that in those days wigs were powdered and after powdering the excess had to be flapped away. It is just possible you may escape that particular task.

'His guide.' He told him where to go and how to get there.

'His stop watch.' He told him when to go.

'His auditor.' He supervised his finances.

'His treasurer.' You, like John Lamb, will always have £20 ready in your hand for when your Principal suddenly says: 'Good Heavens, I've got no money.'

'He did nothing without consulting him.' This is true today, whether the decision is something comparatively trivial or something momentous: 'Ought I to give up this type of work? Am I getting too fat? Ought I to apply to the Lord Chancellor to be made a Queen's Counsel?' The right answer to two at least of these questions depends on whether you have acquired the skill which you ought to have done after this series of lectures.

'Or failed in anything without expecting and fearing his admonishing.' Well, I advise you to go easy on this. Don't start the admonishing tomorrow morning or else your attendance at these lectures may become slightly unnecessary!' Wait about twenty years.

Finally 'He resigned his title almost to respect as a master, if his clerk could ever have forgotten for a moment that he was his servant.' This is most important. It is true of many barristers today. My advice is treasure his friendship by never forgetting your place. Nobody knows where the line is, but you will immediately know if either you or he steps over it. [1971: 3–4]

In sum, these descriptions portray a master-and-servant relationship, with the emphasis on loyalty to the master from his faithful clerk. When we look behind these public utterances, relations between clerk and barrister are not always so anodyne.

CRITIQUES OF THE FORMAL CONCEPTION

In the latter 1960s three main critiques of the official line were published (Zander, 1968; Abel-Smith and Stevens, 1968; Johnstone and Hopson, 1967). All three addressed and emphasised the potential for development of conflict in the clerk–barrister relationship. Zander, the most polemical, wrote, 'the position of the English barrister's clerk is a unique and disturbing one' (1968: 83). And, more important, 'He does have considerable power . . .' (1968: 84). Thus:

The clerk exercises an influence over the distribution of work amongst his supposed principals which is out of all proportion to his qualifications or other attainments. The clerk system has the effect of putting members of the Bar into a position where their careers can be made or marred by the opinion held of them not merely by their clients but by their clerks. Throughout his career a barrister has to watch his step with his clerk. The uneasy relationship is a little like that between the subaltern and the sergeant-major—except that whereas the sergeant-major would himself do the young officer's job, the clerk is completely unqualified to do legal work and that the clerk enjoys greater power over his 'masters' than any sergeant-major. [1968: 85–6]

Abel-Smith and Stevens (1968: 110–11) are more restrained:

Indeed, the barrister's clerk is the pivot of a barrister's practice. The good opinion of the clerk is particularly important for a young barrister in view of the considerable patronage the former can distribute. While technically the young barrister is senior to the clerk, in practice the boot tends to be on the other foot . . . The relationship may even vary according to the method of remunerating the clerk.

Both Zander and Abel-Smith and Stevens suffer from the same fault—they have no empirical data on which to base their assertions. Neither really attempted to discover what the relationship entailed in action, whereas Johnstone and Hopson (1967), while not fully setting forth their methodology, offered a more comprehensive account:[8]

Relations of barristers' clerks with different categories in chambers is subtle and varied. Socially they are inferior to even the most junior barristers: they do not lunch with counsel, fraternise with them outside working hours, or belong to the Inns or the same clubs, and in general are considered as belonging to a different and lower class. But their control over work flow and fees, and to some extent their frequent long association with the chambers, gives them great power and status that are recognised by the barristers in their chambers. [1967: 434]

Johnstone and Hopson have widened the scope and introduced a human element. The discrepant roles of clerk and barrister are seen to emanate from their respective class differences. But still, as with all these descriptions, there is a lack of detailed empirical data.

FROM INDIVIDUALS TO COLLECTIVITIES

In the decade 1965–75 the Bar doubled in size from 2,164 to 4,263 but the number of chambers has not risen in proportion to the number of barristers.[9] In London the increase in sets has been slight, approximately eight per cent. Instead chambers have expanded in size, the average number in a set being around fifteen barristers. This is radically different from the pre-1914 era, when a clerk served one or two barristers only.

Technically, as Boulton (1975: 54) shows, the individual orientation of the clerk to the barrister still prevails, for the clerk contracts with each barrister separately. However, his perception of the chambers has radically altered. He thinks of it as a collective unit, capable of providing a service at all levels of expertise from the greenhorn pupil to the authoritative Queen's Counsel. The clerk refers to this as the 'ladder' in his chambers, the balanced unit of barristers. Balance is important; to be out of balance usually means the chambers have too much tail. It is on the basis of the chambers being in equipoise and thus providing a complete range of services that the clerk makes his appeal to the solicitor clients.

This shift in the structure of the chambers system—from the workplace of the individual to a quasi-corporate organisation—has brought forth a corresponding response in the clerk. Officialdom, however, demands that he retain at least the appearance of the pre-1914 individual orientation. So the clerk concerns himself with the welfare and profitability of the individual, but only in so far as the individual does not impede the progress of the collectivity. One senior expressed his difficulties thus: 'I have to wear twenty-five hats, one for each member of chambers, because they're all different and you have to know how to deal with them; a versatile personality is required.' Another referred to 'the way I have to deal with twenty-three prima-donnas'.

CHARACTERISTICS OF FACE-TO-FACE INTERACTION[10]

The central feature of encounters is that they consist of face-to-face interaction (see Goffman, 1964); the clerk's goal is to define and manage his encounters with his barristers.

The clerk generally takes the initiative in defining the situation through his mode of address. He calls the barrister 'Sir' or 'Mr Blank'; rarely does he call him by his first name.[11] The barrister, age and seniority notwithstanding, responds with his clerk's christian name. This simple yet profound ritual immediately determines the social distance between them; each knows his 'place'. Goffman writes, 'and of course, in scrupulously observing the proper forms he may find that he is free to insinuate all kinds of disregard by carefully modifying intonation, pronunciation, pacing, and so forth' (1956: 478). But for the most part in the everyday course of things the clerk's use of 'Sir' is, superficially, of no serious consequence. It can even be a convenience. Occasionally, a senior clerk noted, one can temporarily forget the name of the barrister (especially the pupils) and the impersonal 'Sir' provides the necessary escape. In less conventionally organised sets of chambers, however, these symbols of deference are eschewed in favour of first-name terms. And there are times in the more traditional sets of chambers when the formal address is not used. Part-time staff, such as accounts clerks, and 'girls' (typists) who are not fully socialised in the same way tend to resent having to defer and sometimes call barristers by their first names.

The rank of the barrister is crucial in determining the character of the clerk's behaviour towards him. The extremes of attention and inattention are revealed during encounters with the head of chambers and with a pupil. Pupils enter the clerk's purview only when they become economically viable. Even then their temporary situation commands a different response from the clerk, for they may be *in* the chambers but they are not *of* it. As a result, the clerk may be more overbearing with the pupils than with a member. In one set of chambers, for example, the pupils lived in fear of the senior clerk's blustering manner, whereas the head of chambers always received courteous treatment. For instance, when the head of chambers attended court in London the senior clerk would accompany him, carrying the barrister's robes in the bag, the 'boy' bringing up the rear with the books and papers. In the case of a pupil the clerk's 'Sir' can be offhand or dismissive, a superficial deference; with the head of chambers it is generally used with sincerity and, on occasion, reverence.

This stratification of the chambers provides the clerk with a model against which he can regulate his actions *vis-à-vis* his barristers. He will acknowledge a new pupil's presence merely as another 'object' in the chambers. If children should be seen but not heard, pupils should be neither seen nor heard. This attitude was openly displayed in one set of chambers:

1. Do not use the phones between four and six p.m. [the busiest time of day].
2. No private telephone calls are allowed.
3. Help to bring back the pupil-master's books from the court.

4. Do not use the kitchen.[12]

The pupil was deemed to be the responsibility of the pupil-master rather than the clerk.

After the first six months of pupilage the status of the pupil changes—he becomes a potential unit in the workforce. The clerk may present him with his first brief. The occasion is of negligible importance to the clerk, it is just a matter of another barrister being available to do a remand or bail application and one less brief to return. For the pupil it is of symbolic importance. He is beginning his practice as a barrister. It can take on the idealised aspects of a prize-giving ceremony: on one occasion a pupil entered the clerks' room with his pupil-master, the clerk strode across to them, proffered a brief and shook the pupil by the hand vigorously, saying, 'Congratulations, sir. I wish you the best of luck.'

Giving pupils small cases serves a twofold purpose. The clerk has another barrister to cope with the minor work, and it provides an opportunity to test the novitiate. Most chambers prefer to choose future members from their stock of pupils. 'Better the devil you know,' as one clerk said. But this type of selection generally occurs only in criminal and common law chambers, where pupils can handle work considered suitable for an inexperienced barrister. Civil litigation is more complex and is reserved for members of the chambers. Although some drafting of particulars or an opinion may be given to a pupil, this is a direct transaction between pupil-master and pupil without the intervention of the clerk (i.e. 'devilling').

The main difference between a pupil in his second six months and a newly tenanted member of chambers is the priority the latter has in the receipt of work, though there is no essential difference in the class of work each does. But acquiring a practice is a drawn-out process, and at this stage the new tenant is heavily dependent on the clerk to generate work for him. A young barrister must be flexible and accept any type of case whatever his preferences. He may be unwilling to act as prosecutor, a disinclination he would be expected to contain or conceal if such work were distributed to the chambers. The more specialised the work, e.g. tax or planning law, the longer the neophyte must wait to receive a share. Two or three years is not unusual; until then he must 'devil' (i.e. substitute) for others, forgoing the opportunity to sign, and get the credit for, the papers returned to the client.

When a barrister is being launched in his career (and after), especially in common law and criminal law, and to a lesser extent in civil law chambers, clerks prefer to have him in court where he is most visible to those whose opinions count—solicitors and clients. Extended absences compel clerk and barrister to communicate by telephone. Most chambers require their members to ring the clerk at least twice a day. The clerk knows where his barristers are and can tell them where to go and what to do when adjustments have to be made in their schedules. Offenders who forget incur their clerk's wrath, because he cannot organise their schedules properly. Some clerks will even express open annoyance. One senior insisted on two persistent offenders being censured by the chambers as a whole. Another refused to speak to a barrister because the latter had missed a magistrates' court case through failing to ring in at midday.

Besides appearing in court and keeping the clerk informed of his whereabouts, the barrister must be punctual. Whereas an absent barrister can be replaced, incidentally creating an impression that the clerk is saving the day for the client, one who is late only succeeds in disgracing the clerk in the eyes of solicitor and client. For example, one young barrister was late at court three times in one week. The first time he was able to excuse himself with an apology, as his case had not come on immediately at 10.30 a.m. (the starting time for most courts). On the following two occasions he missed the start of his case, which had to be put back in the lists, resulting in angry solicitors telephoning the clerk to know why their barrister had failed to appear on time. The barrister's excuses were that his car had broken down and that he had forgotten to put his clock forward for summer time (he claimed he was 'really on time'). When it was explained to him that solicitors would not instruct unreliable counsel—the implication being that the clerk would be reluctant to give him briefs—the man was never late again.

Early in a barrister's career the clerk is crucial to the development of his practice. As the practice becomes self-sustaining the clerk's influence diminishes. Relations will become strained if the barrister takes advantage of this lessening of dependence. Two examples illustrate the point.

At 5.20 p.m. a barrister of thirteen years' call informed her clerk she wouldn't be able to do a case the next day because her teeth needed some urgent treatment. The clerk tried to persuade her to postpone the dental appointment because of the difficulty of finding a substitute at such short notice. He knew it was not pressing, as he had noted it in the diary several weeks earlier. She insisted he find another barrister. To begin with, the solicitor rejected alternatives from the same chambers. After trying elsewhere the clerk reluctantly rang the solicitor. 'Arnold, I'm very sorry, and a bit annoyed as well, but she's in great pain and can't do the case. I want you to know it's the fault of counsel and not the clerks' room. Look, I've phoned round the strong sets, but no joy, and I don't want to go to sets you don't know because something might go wrong. Well, you can have X., Y. or Z . . . OK, Y. Sorry about this, Arnold.' After this the barrister entered the clerks' room and heard the result. 'Thanks, George, I'll buy you a drink some time.' The clerk, however, only wanted her to telephone the solicitor and apologise herself.

Over the course of a complex and protracted prosecution the leading barrister, a QC, supported by two junior barristers from his chambers, was getting more and more irritable over the delays. One of the juniors was occasionally able to take time off to argue another case in the Appeal Court. The clerk had already refused two briefs on behalf of the other one because of the prosecution. Although this barrister was earning a good fee, extended involvement in the case was affecting his practice. To prevent further decline, his clerk persuaded the QC to release him for a one-day case in the Crown Court. But when the day arrived the leader was more cantankerous than usual and bluntly refused his junior permission to leave: a substitute would have to be found. The clerk was powerless to change the QC's mind.

Occasionally, however, clerks can exert some pressure. When a simple opinion had to be drafted quickly the only barrister available was a senior counsel who baulked at a task he considered beneath his status. But the clerk insisted, pointing out that there was nobody else in the chambers to do it, and as it had to be given to the solicitor the next day. Afterwards the clerk joked about it, allowing the barrister to save face.

Certain activities—fee-fixing and the listing and scheduling of cases—are left to the clerk, or almost. Sometimes clerk and barrister disagree, each wishing to take control, and the clerk will face a struggle. If he can afford to be indulgent in the matter of fees, he will. It is always good for business, whatever the barrister's wishes. In one case a barrister who, because of his political leanings, undertook

many welfare cases expressed concern about charging a fee for a
conference and opinion, as the client was paying his own costs and
had an incompetent solicitor. Here the clerk could be indulgent and
reduce the fee because the barrister handled enough work to carry an
occasional reduction. But the clerk does not always accept the
barrister's inclination so readily. In a case which involved drafting a
long and complex affidavit the clerk decided to charge £35. The
barrister objected strongly, saying that it should be £55 because of
the amount of time he had spent drafting and redrafting the affidavit.
The clerk was adamant. 'No, *I* fix the fee, and this is what it will be,'
a decision the barrister eventually accepted.[13] But where a barrister's
specialism was particularly esoteric and complicated both the clerk
and the barrister had to calculate the fees, and send out the fee notes,
which they would do periodically when the barrister felt he was
short of funds.

Lists are also the preserve of the clerk. Normally he consults his
barristers only when a problem has arisen, for example through
'going part-heard' (i.e. a case continuing to another day). When a
barrister went part-heard, and was unable to start a case the next
morning, he and the clerk discussed who should stand in for an hour
while the first case finished. The clerk suggested another barrister in
the chambers who was free and had experience in the type of case. He
was rejected out of hand as too old and decrepit. Ultimately the
barrister's view prevailed and the clerk had to find another
alternative, even though it made managing the diary more difficult.
Cases frequently go part-heard on the judgement, requiring the
barrister to return to the courtroom the next day just to hear the
judge's decision. In these instances a clerk will substitute a younger
barrister if the senior can be more profitably deployed elsewhere.

It is, however, barely pardonable for a barrister to agree a date for
a hearing without consulting his clerk. When a barrister returned
from a Crown Court where his case had been adjourned for
sentence, he told his clerk that he had agreed a date for the sentence.
The clerk was furious, because it clashed with a long-standing
county court case. 'You want me to shift it, I suppose?' He was all the
more angry because he knew the barrister had been too scared of the
judge to say that he needed to consult his clerk before he could fix a
date. In another instance a barrister went further and agreed a date,
without the clerk's knowledge, for a different barrister. The clerk
was livid, but could only change the date, and embarrass the

barrister, for his stupidity, in front of others. The opposite would also happen. For example, a barrister who had an overloaded day—a case at a provincial court, and four undefended divorces and two other cases in London—asked his clerk's advice about which ones to do. He felt more responsible for the provincial case, as it had been longer in the diary, but the clerk preferred him to do the London ones. More solicitors and clients would be appeased. He was persuaded to let the provincial case be returned (it was given to a pupil).

As a junior barrister extends and consolidates his practice he is able to assert independence of the power of the clerk. But the dependency ratio alters again with the question of taking silk and becoming Queen's Counsel. The decision to apply for the 'letters patent' is a matter for careful discussion between clerk and barrister. Taking silk can be like starting at the Bar all over again. The change in the type of work and the size of the fees demands a complete restructuring of the practice.

Greater deference is generally shown to silks than to other barristers; Queen's Counsel can raise the status of the chambers considerably.[14] In one set of chambers with seven QCs the senior clerk devoted his time entirely to their welfare, leaving his first junior to clerk the junior barristers. The relationship between the clerk and the silk is close, especially if he is head of chambers, as a result of the length of time they have been together. They form the main axis of power. In many chambers the administrative expenses and rent are apportioned by the senior clerk and head of chambers (other sets use a committee system). Some sets are arranged on more despotic lines where the head of chambers and clerk decide, without consulting any members, the amounts to be contributed to expenses.

As noted above, the senior clerk accompanies his head of chambers to court, dresses him in the robing room, and sometimes watches him in court. Some clerks even accompany their silk overseas. One travelled regularly to Singapore and Hong Kong with his head of chambers, who had a busy practice there. Another went to Bermuda with his head of chambers, a trip he managed to convert into a holiday. On such journeys the clerk provides moral support while taking care of travel and other arrangements.

Eccentricities are tolerated more in silks. One QC addressed all his clerks as Charles, regardless of their real name. In another case a head

of chambers was attending a conference in Germany over the
weekend and told his clerk to buy a plane ticket. Two days after his
expected return the silk was due to have a consultation with a client.
Four alterations were made to the flight timetable by the silk, two to
the outward journey and two to the return. His clerk was extremely
annoyed—'He can never make up his bloody mind.' The final
alteration to the return journey entailed postponing the consultation,
to the exasperation of the solicitor. Rearranging consultations for
this silk was the bane of the clerk's life. One week the silk had two
consultations, on Wednesday and the following Friday. First the
barrister changed his Friday consultation to the Saturday, causing
the clerk only slight annoyance. Then he asked for the Wednesday
one to be postponed for a week. This upset the clerk, moreover the
solicitor refused any alteration and demanded the return of the brief.
The clerk complained to the 'deputy' head of chambers, his other
silk. 'Sir, he's so selfish, he really must be told that he can't treat
clients like this.' When the head of chambers heard that he might lose
the brief he immediately agreed to the original time. Later the same
day he telephoned to have the Saturday consultation moved from 11
a.m. to 9 a.m. The clerk refused, explaining that the clients would
never accept an appointment so early. Nevertheless he was worried
in case the silk failed to turn up. In fact he arrived late on Wednesday
(fortunately the clients were late as well), and his clerk scolded him
publicly for his selfish and uncompromising behaviour. After the
consultation the clerk resumed his normal deferential behaviour.

A delicate problem for any clerk is that of a barrister's failure.
Failure can be measured by the distortion in the career timetable.
Career timetables at the Bar are organised on a cohort system; twice
a year barristers are called to the Bar. A barrister can measure the
progress of his career against that of his contemporaries (see Roth,
1963: 93–114). The high visibility to others allows the process to be
measured with some accuracy. Failure to achieve a progressively
rising career, e.g. taking silk at forty-five or thereabouts, requires
the clerk to attenuate the disappointment, and either persuade the
barrister to revise his expectations or encourage him in his original
aspirations. Goffman describes it as 'cooling the mark out':

For the mark, cooling represents a process of adjustment to an impossible
situation—a situation arising from having defined himself in a way which
the social facts contradict. The mark must therefore be supplied with a new
set of apologies for himself, a new framework in which to see himself and

judge himself. A process of redefining the self along defensible lines must be instigated and carried along; since the mark himself is frequently in too weakened a condition to do this, the cooler must initially do it for him. [1952: 456]

'Cooling' is illustrated by the predicament of colonial QCs who must revert to junior counsel on returning to England. One man who had failed three years running in his application for silk complained bitterly to his clerk about the injustice of the system. The clerk knew that he was below the required standard, but cushioned the barrister's failure with the excuse that the Lord Chancellor would be inundated if he nominated silks from ex-colonials. This not only soothed the barrister's feelings but saved some of his self-esteem as well. Another barrister, who had specialised in landlord and tenant law, believed his practice was not succeeding and tried to persuade his clerk that he ought to broaden his field to include criminal law. The clerk knew that any such move would spoil the barrister's opportunity of ever regaining his specialism,[15] and insisted he persevere even if it meant temporary hardship. Three months later the barrister was pleased at having earned £600 in one week.

As Goffman (1952: 457) puts it: 'A related way of handling the mark is to offer him another chance to qualify for the role at which he has failed. After his fall from grace, he is allowed to retrace his steps and try again.' The clerk may sometimes be over-protective towards his principals when he considers they may be deviating from the implied norm. Take the example of a barrister who had argued with a stipendiary magistrate over a procedural point where he felt the magistrate was quite wrong. He decided to write to the magistrate, formally registering a complaint, and send an explanatory note to the solicitors. The clerk questioned the wisdom of this, lest the barrister 'lose face'. The barrister, however, was resolute. A senior member of chambers reassured the clerk that the proposal was proper, but the clerk remained sceptical.

BACKGROUND EXPECTATIONS, ATTITUDES AND REALITIES

Up front, the situation between clerk and barrister is fairly well defined—the clerk acts, for the most part, in a deferential, controlled manner. Backstage behaviour and attitudes are characterised by ambivalence, or, as one clerk put it, 'clerks and counsel have a love–hate relationship'. It is here that the incipient tensions and conflict hinted at up front are revealed. Moreover the team structure of clerks within the confines of the backstage is emphasised; clerks will support each other in disputes against barristers.

The tension of the love–hate relationship does find expression through the clerks' evaluation of the barristers; they generally base their judgement on the assumptions that barristers have no common sense and that they are lazy. A common law clerk explained, 'I tell you, barristers need clerks, because they've got no common sense, and that's what a clerk's got. These barristers go to university and they get pumped full of law through one ear and their common sense comes dripping out the other side' (said replete with gestures—fingers in at one ear and the others waving away from the other). This is in sharp contrast to the formal view: 'Those who . . . found themselves selected as senior clerks had had the additional advantage of being thrown into daily contact with members of the Bar, men and women of erudition and ability whose professional conduct is at the highest level.' (Newland, 1971: 2) Another clerk said of his barristers, 'Some of the suggestions they come up with for running the chambers would have us bankrupt within a week. A clerk can't learn the trade, like a barrister does; that's why this educational thing is a load of crap.'

Laziness, the second assumption, is the opposite of what a clerk expects and demands from a barrister—hard work. No clerk likes to see his chambers carrying someone who is not contributing to its work load. When a barrister told his clerk that he wouldn't work that afternoon because he had a bad back, the clerk's opinion was, 'He's skiving.' Another was criticised as irresponsible for taking time off to attend a children's party 'when he's got *so much* work to do'.

Hard work is always of prime importance to the clerk. A former QC who had been appointed to the Bench was much admired by his clerk, who described him as one of the most eminent QCs at the Chancery Bar, always inundated with work and spending most of his time in court. He would hold consultations at 9 a.m., then go into court; at lunchtime he would have a sandwich while working on other matters; after lunch he would be back in court, then he would rush back to chambers for more consultations, and finally return home to more paperwork. 'His notes were so well prepared that you or I could have done the case, he'd find every authority to cover every possible point.' If a barrister is held in high enough esteem some degree of laziness may be grudgingly accepted. 'He has a good brain, and the Lord Chief [Justice] loves him, but he's lazy. I've just got to put up with it, he'll never change.' The cause of laziness like this, according to an experienced common law clerk, was that some barristers had always had *too much* work, never having had to build a practice up laboriously over the years.

There is an obvious contradiction here. On one hand the clerk wants economic success for his chambers; on the other he regrets having to forgo some influence over his 'governors' because of their high turnover of work. Some of the older clerks find the contradiction hard to accept, especially as they started when the influence of the clerk was substantially greater.[16] An extension of this attitude is found in the distinction some of them drew between barristers of the 'old' school and the 'new'. Those of the 'new' school were the idle ones: they would do what suited them, without considering the problems for their clerks. Barristers of the old school were 'clerks' men', gentlemen, who treated their clerk with respect. There is probably more than a touch of nostalgia in such memories. One clerk remembered appointment to a senior clerkship at the age of nineteen, soon after the first world war. 'The head of chambers wanted a clerk he could mould instead of a clerk moulding him.' But there was a tendency among some of the older barristers to rely heavily on their clerks. Thus one Queen's Counsel, wanting a day off: 'Look, George, I think I've done quite well today. Do you think I could have tomorrow off?' One clerk, who had a mixture of old and new schools in his set, was fond of one particular barrister who had been with him for twenty years. 'Every set of chambers ought to have a person like Mr Smith. He's very honest but just a bit selfish.' This man was also wealthy and made few demands on his clerk to collect fees and the like.

The love–hate relationship is brought further into relief by the way in which clerks react to deviation from their ideal type. Lack of common sense and laziness are general attributes; there are, however, more specific ones. One clerk, for example, was embarrassed that his chambers were thought of as left-wing, and would try to deny it, even though some of the members belonged to, or had belonged to, the Communist Party. He maintained it was a fiction that in some ways was good for business and in others bad. For example, his head of chambers had not been appointed to the

Bench—good. But neither did his chambers get prosecution work for the Attorney General—bad. Perhaps the most common deviation from the ideal concerned women barristers.[17] The general view held they were useful for family law work, divorces or cases involving children, but not heavy criminal or financial ones. A clerk explained his view of women thus:

> Women aren't physically or emotionally suited to the Bar; they're not as robust as men. It's something to do with their glands. They get too involved. I've got one female barrister—took her on because I thought she would add a bit of glamour to the chambers. But after two years I've realised my mistake. If she writes an opinion she'll take twenty pages instead of three, and I can't charge the solicitor for that.
>
> I have a young barrister who's good—he tells the solicitor what he wants to know, he doesn't try to prove to the solicitor that he knows all the law, like she does.
>
> The other day she came to see me after being in court and rabbited on. I was taking phone calls and ignored her. After twenty minutes she said, 'Oh, the solicitor would like the fee note quickly' [in a falsetto voice]. And I said, 'That's the first thing of merit you've said in this conversation.' She said, 'I thought you might see it that way' [falsetto] and left the room. Ten minutes later she was back asking what the fee was. All she *really* cared about was the money.

There are infrequent occasions when young women barristers are accepted into the clerks' company for an evening and treated *almost* as if they were not barristers. One clerk once got his barrister very drunk, but still called her 'Miss'. Clerks avoid emotional or sexual involvement with their female barristers, because they believe the relationship would lead to some kind of 'aggravation' (trouble).[18] Despite this prejudice, if a female barrister is successful the clerk is satisfied. A common law clerk to a woman barrister of the middle range with a thriving matrimonial practice said, 'When Miss Brown started, she was hopeless, but look how she's turned out. Great!' As though in confirmation this barrister once confided to him that she thought she was earning almost an 'obscene' amount of money; she had just noticed that she had earned more in one week than during her first year at the Bar.

Barristers who belong to ethnic minorities can also suffer from a clerk's prejudice. A young black barrister in a busy set of chambers discovered he was taking twice as long as his contemporaries to build up a practice, the reason being that the clerk was not referring much work to him.[19] When he began to be more successful, the clerk's prejudice began to fade (at least in business terms). In another set of chambers an Asian of some years' call was taken on only as a door tenant or 'squatter';[20] the clerks did not want him as a tenant. A common law clerk who, for a time, had had some Greek barristers in his chambers swore he would never clerk for them or their like again, because they gave him 'too much aggravation': their main fault was late payment of clerks' fees. Most other clerks escaped the problem by not admitting barristers of ethnic minorities as members of chambers.[21]

Married men—those in their late twenties and early thirties—cause some concern. This is generally the time when a barrister starts accumulating commitments—a wife, a mortgage and other necessities and luxuries of life. Ideally the clerk would prefer him to remain without such responsibilities for the first ten or twelve years of practice so that his energies can be directed entirely to the law and the chambers. A new pupil in one set was actually felt to have made the wrong choice in coming to the Bar because he had a wife, children and a mortgage. The same clerk was perturbed to learn that two of his successful young barristers were taking on extra commitments: one was buying his first house, the other was moving to a larger one. It led to an unhealthy preoccupation with the demands on one's income, according to the clerk, and sometimes an equally 'unhealthy' belief that the clerk was perhaps earning too much, so that delay in paying his fees was likely.

Criticisms of this type would arise in the clerks' room when something went wrong. A middle-level barrister discovered that he was double-booked on the same day at different courts. The senior clerk said, 'He gets us to do all this [sorting things out], but trying to get money out of him is like getting blood out of a stone. They never pay. They go on about what I earn, but I never get anything from them. Even A. has lent my money to his brother.' The junior clerk joined in: 'The younger ones pay up all right, but the others—*terrible*.' To which the senior clerk added, 'You build up their practice over the years, then they come in and tell you they're going to set up their own chambers without giving you the three months' notice they're supposed to. And they just give you a bit of silver worth fifteen quid when you could have got over a hundred quid normally. It's disgraceful.'

'Take X. He's very accommodating, but how many solicitors did he bring with him?' The junior clerk managed to recall an instance, but the senior went on, 'How many did Y. bring? *None.* How many did Z. bring? *None.* They think they're God's gift, but they bring *nothing* with them. We supply them with the solicitors, then they don't want to pay us. I wonder how much we'd get if we were entertainment managers. More, probably.'

Occasionally clerks are burdened with elderly, unproductive barristers—people with a private income who make pathetic attempts to appear competent and productive but in reality do no more than the occasional magistrates' court case. The clerks defer to them, as they do to their other governors, but their real aim is to be rid of them, because they do not repay the effort of finding them an occasional case and collecting the fee. In short, they are uneconomic. One clerk had an elderly barrister in his chambers who would come in once every few weeks to collect any cheques that might be waiting for him. He never spent any time in the chambers, but had a room whose only alternative use was to accommodate the accounts clerk. The senior was waiting for the day when the man retired and he could put the room to better use. 'I can put at least two men in there,' he said. Another clerk in a similar predicament solved it by issuing a serious final demand for his fees, which compelled the barrister to change chambers.

Alcohol is integral to the functioning of the legal profession. The extreme pressure of work, or conversely insufficient work, provides the impetus to alcoholism. Fundamentally, to the clerk it is a question of degree. If a governor is still working satisfactorily he will not interfere. One clerk remembered, with affection, several barristers who used to get drunk in the afternoon, then snooze in a governor's room till the pubs reopened. However, a junior clerk in one set was desperately seeking another post because 'half my governors are alcoholics', and business had been suffering as a result. A civil law clerk reported, 'I had one governor who worked so hard he had a breakdown and became an alcoholic and it finished him—he had to go into hospital.' Solving the crises of alcoholic governors gives rise to the same difficulties as with other problem governors. What is the best way of removing unwanted barristers from the chambers if it comes to that? The clerk has three options. He can do nothing and hope that the other governors will take action. He can enlist the support of a faction within the chambers; or he can attempt to remove the man himself. The 'easing out' of a governor will be discussed later.

Every clerk has a mental picture of what he considers to be the ideal barrister. Two qualities have been mentioned, diligence and obedience—although one clerk found it difficult to define the right qualities, as he just 'knew' whether a man was 'right' or not by looking at him. But a rank order of qualities may be constructed: personality, diligence, obedience, intellect. (In certain specialisms intellect may carry a higher rating, but it is never at the top of the scale). Thus barristers must have the sort of personality that will impress solicitors and clients and induce them to continue briefing the chambers. One clerk looked for a calm, tidy, firm and commanding personality which was neither aggressive nor meek. One barrister who was unduly shy was advised to quit the Bar, as he did not inspire confidence. Another clerk was prepared to take a barrister on only as a squatter, because 'He's too nervous to have as a member'. In a newly established chambers the clerk favoured the barrister with the greatest self-assurance and made sure that new clients met him first.

The personality of the barrister must be malleable enough to respond to the directions of the clerk where chambers matters are concerned—for example, the ordinance that barristers must telephone at least twice a day to inform the clerk of their whereabouts. This requirement is adhered to more rigorously in common law sets than in civil and Chancery chambers.[22] In one recently formed set the clerk was obliged to reprimand a young barrister who deemed it a tedious duty beneath his dignity. Implicit in the clerk's warning, however, was the threat that there would be less work for him unless his attitude changed. Another clerk had a persistent non-telephoner whom he called 'a silly sod'; 'he's always doing this'. Sometimes, forgetting to remain in contact can mean the barrister not arriving at court on time. Such absentmindedness, in the clerk's view, is damaging to his reputation with solicitors and clients. Even if the offenders are a small minority in the chambers the effect can spill over compounding the harm.

Intellectual ability is not in itself enough to outweigh defects of personality. As a first junior clerk said, a barrister 'might have a First from Cambridge but still be useless'. In the tax and Chancery specialisms intellect is at a higher premium. One clerk thought that only those who got a First or Upper Second in the Bar finals were worth considering.[23] In these specialisms the emphasis is on interpreting the law, whereas in criminal work it is on advocacy.

Good advocacy—which, according to some clerks, contains no law—depends on strong personality and adroitness of mind so as to create a good impression in court. Occasionally a clerk will watch one of his governors performing. His interest lies in the interplay of personalities and the number of victories his governor scores, or how well he is defeated. It is unnecessary for him to observe his governors continually, as the rate at which they are briefed by solicitors is the indicator of success.[24] The clerk's reaction to their qualities and defects is shown in the way he manages them.

This is one of his central tasks, and one of the most demanding ones. He must be able to control wayward barristers or he will not be able to do his job. A clerk who entered the Temple before the war adopted a paternalistic attitude:

> You have to be careful, dealing with barristers: you need patience, tolerance and understanding. The moulding of a barrister is a very delicate operation. I like nothing better than to see a young man start and then go to the Bench.
>
> Our pupils don't really work until they've done twelve months with us. If you put them into court after six months, just in magistrates' courts, it doesn't really do their careers any good. They need to be able to show themselves—to learn.
>
> I just deal in crime, I don't like civil work. At one time we used to do a lot of Western Circuit work, so if I had to send a barrister out I used to check with his wife first to see if she minded. She might say, 'Is it good for his career?' I would say it was, and the answer would be, 'Then send him.' When I told the barrister he was going, he'd get alarmed and worry about leaving his wife, and of course I'd say, 'It's all right, sir, I've checked with your wife and she doesn't mind,' and off he'd go.
>
> You need to be a psychiatrist and psychologist for this job. When I went in to the war I spent three and a half years in a prisoner-of-war camp. It taught me a lot about human character and has stayed with me ever since. I can judge a man very well now: I listen to him and I can tell if he's arrogant or got that certain something that means he'll do well. If a barrister's going to be successful he's got to work hard. Now, for example, I've always had Treasury counsel in my chambers. Being a senior Treasury counsel really means seeing your children only at dinner time. One of my governors, for example, had to return the [. . .] case because he was working on the [. . .] case. They have to read mountains of papers and work all hours, including Saturdays and Sundays. It's the kind of job that can kill them or make them very ill.

The quality of this avowed concern for a barrister can vary widely. A pupil in her second six months had been seconded to another set of chambers for a week and came in to tell the clerk she was back. The clerk looked her up and down and said, 'Yes, miss. Fine, miss.' When she had gone he turned to the others and asked, 'Who's she?' He could not even remember his own pupils. Another clerk, who tended to leave the bulk of his work to his junior, once accosted a young barrister in the Great Hall of the Law Courts with, 'Now don't tell me: I know the face. Don't tell me,' etc. Eventually the barrister lost patience and replied, 'You *should* know me. You've been my clerk for nine months.'

One of the clerk's main activities in handling his governors is coping with their personal affairs. A clerk mentioned that his barristers came to him with all types of problems, some very embarrassing, 'but they've got to get these things off their chest and it might as well be to me. It's part of the job.' Another remarked, 'I can guarantee getting at least four phone calls over the weekend from my governors, from nine o'clock in the morning on Saturday to midnight Sunday.' The problems range from marital to career difficulties.[25]

Career difficulties are the most common, and the easiest to deal with. For example, a clerk had two women barristers who did a substantial amount of industrial tribunal work.

They're always there, but it's not good for them. It's a dead end, because it means they're not expanding their practices. One of them's really keen on banking law, and she can't do this kind of work at the present time. It's very difficult for me to switch them from it on to the better work, because I can't upset the solicitors, but I do know they shouldn't be doing this work now, with their call. One woman I've got works tremendously hard. In fact I've several who do, and they don't leave chambers until eight or nine at night. Now this woman is having six weeks' holiday this summer, and she needs every day of it, otherwise she'd crack up with the pressure of work. It's very important to gauge how hard you can let your barristers work.

The clerk, then, has to steer his barristers through a welter of conflicts, creating an environment in which they can perform efficiently, to the benefit of both the chambers and the clerk. By quietly manipulating unseen strings the clerk prompts and restrains his governors' behaviour—what Lukes (1974: 22) has aptly described as 'controlling the agenda'.

In the case of clerk and barrister this is definitely so; the barrister, to a great extent, hands over the responsibility for his welfare. The clerk controls the negotiation of fees, the distribution of a considerable portion of the work, and the extent to which he sells or furthers a barrister's career. Knowledge of his strengths and weaknesses enables the clerk to develop a 'career timetable' for him: the type of work he should be doing, the type of court he should be appearing in, and his rate of progress. One clerk tried his utmost to push two young 'high-flyers' who had impressed him by joining the Bar 'cold', without family connections, and one of whom as a pupil had approached the senior clerk first about being taken on by the chambers. A civil law clerk who had a young silk in his thirties with whom he was greatly impressed, predicted that within fifteen years he would be in the House of Lords. When a clerk finds he has a barrister who works hard and successfully he can help him modify the timing of his career—moving him on to heavier work, and perhaps advising him to apply early for silk. Conversely, he protects governors who need restraining from overreaching themselves. For example, a clerk was contacted by another with a returned brief to refer. The only criterion was that the case be handled by a black barrister. The clerk had a black barrister in his chambers but he was not very experienced, and the brief was refused. The black barrister's clerk never consulted him; he refused the brief because it could have made his governor, and hence himself, appear foolish in court. On another occasion a clerk received some papers for a particular barrister on a planning matter. He decided that it was not only outside the man's field, but that he was not yet experienced enough to take on that kind of work. There was another barrister in the chambers who used to be employed by a local authority, and he decided to transfer the papers to him. The solicitor agreed to the change, and, again, neither of the barristers was told what had happened.

Such behaviour is disturbing to barristers when they come face to face with it. Thus a senior who clerked two sets of chambers, one provincial, the other in London, came under heavy criticism from his London barristers when they discovered he was 'returning' briefs from the London to the provincial set. They believed he was being disloyal to the original chambers in the capital and threatened to reduce his percentage commission. Usually clerks are able to prevent their governors from finding out about these backstage manipulations. They generally enjoy sufficient freedom or lack of interference to plan their governors' careers. However, one clerk came close to resigning when his judgement was questioned and rejected. A barrister whom the clerk considered a 'high-flier', was refused a tenancy after completing his pupilage because several of the members objected to him on personal grounds: he did not fit in socially. For a year the clerk kept the man out of the limelight by taking him on as a floater. He was convinced that in time the objectors would relent and allow the floater to join the chambers. On this basis he put the barrister's name in the *Solicitors' Diary* (as apposed to the *Law List*). 'As soon as I mention a barrister's name I know the solicitor will look him up in the *Diary,* so it was worth doing. It was a risk, but none of the barristers were likely to see his name, and if they did I'd have claimed it was a mistake.' After a year the objectors were still holding out firmly. The clerk enlisted support from some other members and the head of chambers, and, finally, when he threatened to resign, the objectors were outvoted.[26] The clerk felt vindicated when the barrister earned £8,000 to £9,000 in his first year.

Thus the extent to which a clerk can construct a 'career timetable' depends on the strength of cohesion with the chambers. Where the outlook is individualistic and non-cohesive the clerk is less constrained, but where there is consensus his freedom is reduced. Hence when it was felt, in a collectively oriented set of chambers, that a black barrister was being discriminated against and given little work by the clerk there was enough pressure to make him change his attitude.

Roth (1963: 105) writes, 'A career timetable is . . . a tight production schedule which not all those following the career path can keep up with.' On occasion the clerk has to reject those who fail to keep up. At the earliest stage this is decided when a pupil is declined a tenancy. Pupil barristers probably suffer most from the ambivalence of the clerk towards his governors. Although future barristers must come from the ranks of pupils, they are a nuisance because the demands they make on the administration are not matched by the return. Thus the pupil's potential for profit is always in the forefront of the clerk's mind. When two pupils entered their second six months in the same set of chambers, the clerks had to decide which of them should start getting work. One of the pupils was acknowledged to be good, by clerks and pupil-master alike, and the pupil-master had asked them to give him something. But he was due to leave in a couple of weeks and was unlikely to come back, so the other one received such briefs as were available. The decision was never explicitly referred to the departing pupil or his pupil-master.

In another instance three young men near the end of their pupilage were planning to establish chambers of their own. Their clerk was to come from one of the chambers' main firms of solicitors. They were hoping that their present clerk would give the new man some training. He was extremely wary of doing so in case he offended the solicitor, and insisted on speaking to the solicitor first. Before he had a chance to do so the pupils changed their plans and joined another chambers. The clerk had escaped an embarrassing situation and loss of 'face'. In general a clerk will try to reduce the shock of transition from pupil to non-tenant by taking the barrister on as a floater or finding him other chambers if he can. But when he offers another clerk a pupil the first question that will be asked is 'What's wrong with him?' One clerk maintained that he could always find a vacancy somewhere if the barrister was not too concerned about status and prestige. In one set of low-status common law chambers the clerk accepted a reject pupil because he was desperate to expand. He was prepared to take a risk and, on being offered the pupil, asked the other clerk's opinion. 'He's f—ing awful to get on with, but he's good.' It turned out to be an accurate diagnosis, and the clerk swore he would never take on someone like that again.

Removing a barrister from the chambers, as opposed to a pupil, is more difficult. Various methods are available. The man can be frankly advised that a different chambers, or career, would be beneficial—advice not usually taken. Or the clerk can enlist the aid of the head of chambers. Usually, however, he approaches the problem in a more discreet manner. One civil law clerk had to deal with a young barrister who had been brought in by the head of chambers. He gave him a few cases to start with, but the barrister failed to attract any return custom. He was never there when needed, always taking time off in pursuit of a second career in music. Neither the clerk nor the head of chambers could induce him to leave, the clerk was forced to stop the flow of work, so finally bringing about his departure.

A barrister in a common law set, blaming his slow progress on the clerk, created disturbances in the clerks' room. In this case aid was invoked from the head of chambers in securing his departure. The clerk characterised him as 'a pain in the arse to clerk', an impression reinforced by the departing barrister's attempt to persuade a colleague to leave with him. A part-time barrister in another chambers was persistently late at court, much to his clerk's annoyance. The problem was compounded by the fact that he was not entirely dependent on the clerk for a livelihood, since one of his relatives was a solicitor. Eventually the senior refused to clerk him, and the man was forced to move to another chambers.[27]

In such cases the clerk first tries to 'cool the mark out'. If that fails he may resort to underhand methods, such as delving into a barrister's background for anything that could be interpreted unfavourably. A clerk who took over a 'bad' set (i.e. one that was not doing much business) found it necessary to remove some five of its members before the chambers' reputation improved. He carried out this operation over a period of two years, since they resisted persuasion, by carefully observing their conduct, making enquiries and listening to gossip. Eventually he had enough information (much of it concerned with touting) to put before the head of chambers with a demand for their expulsion before the gossip spread and invited professional disciplinary action.

The clerk, then, has the power to accelerate or curtail a barrister's career. In this way he builds up his ideal set of chambers, composed of diligent, dutiful barristers. Listening to clerks talk, outside the chambers or within, however, the ideal appears to be rarely if ever attained.

CONCLUSION

The contrast between the clerk's deference to his barrister on the one hand, and his background attitudes towards his governors on the other, is striking. Some official views (Newland, 1971; Cooper, n.d.), and occasionally others, emphasise the degree of trust that should ideally obtain between clerk and barrister. It may be the case with one or two of the barristers in a set (e.g. the head of chambers), but not with the majority. The clerk perceives his governors primarily as economic units to be hired out on a consistently profitable basis. He is aware, however, that his position depends upon maintaining the appearance of good face with his governors. Difficulties must be handled with tact and discretion, and, ideally, the clerk deals with his governor gently so that he avoids further trouble.

Clerks generally have their own ideas as to what constitutes the proper behaviour for a barrister at any given moment in his career and will try to prevent him from deviating from the correct line. Concern for the governors' feelings is one point of correspondence between face-to-face interaction and background attitudes. Yet if other manoeuvres fail the clerk will resort to ways of influencing the barrister's behaviour which show little regard for feelings. He can limit the flow of work or, if that proves difficult, delay collection of their fees.[28]

This control has an historical basis in the development of the legal profession. By absolving themselves of responsibility for negotiating fees and attracting business, barristers surrendered power to their clerks, or rather created a situation in which power would accrue to the clerk. Initially the small size of chambers restricted its exercise, but with the trend towards larger sets the influence of clerks increased correspondingly. At the same time there was a decrease in the 'trust' that obtained between clerk and barrister.[29] That trust was, and still is, symbolised by the form of remuneration, although the trend is towards a reduction from the present norm of 'the clerk's ten per cent' to five or seven per cent.

Face-to-face interaction, then, illustrates the idealised behaviour of the clerk before his governor. But public deference obscures the reality of calculation far short of the strength of feeling that is supposed to exist.

NOTES

1   Goffman (1959) has presented the most elegant synthesis of this approach.
2   Cf. Carlin (1975, 1976), Bankowski and Mungham (1976) and Blumberg (1967).
3   For a critique of Megarry (1962) see Gower (1963).
4   Desmond Ackner, 'The lawyers: in their own defence', *Sunday Times,* 3 November 1968.
5   See chapter 7 for the development of clerks' disciplinary codes and ethical standards.
6   E. Grayson, 'Key law man', *The Observer,* 12 December 1976.
7   Evidence of the Senate of the Inns of Court and the Bar; Section III, A.2.3, (a), (c), (e).
8   The footnotes on pp. 426–7 indicate that they visited and spoke to the individuals in sets of chambers.
9   The following table is from Benson (1979: I, 453, table 33.6):

Growth in numbers of barristers and chambers, 1965–78

	1965	1978
Numbers of barristers in practice[a]	2,164	4,263
Numbers of new entrants[b]	138	285
Numbers of sets of chambers[a]	256	302
London	181	197
Provinces	75	105
Average number of barristers per set	8	14

a Number at 1 October of year shown.
b Number entering during calendar year ended 30 September of year shown.

10   In his discussion of the dramaturgical perspective Goffman considers the regions or stage where the interaction takes place: 'A region may be defined as any place that is bounded to some degree by barriers to perception' (1959: 109). And he divides the region into frontstage and backstage. Frontstage is where performer and audience participate in a mannered ritual which displays the morally evaluative content of their relationships to others. The frontstage performance is an idealised view in which the setting (the props on the stage), appearance and manner of the performers are carefully controlled. Conversely, the 'backstage may be defined as a place, relative to a given performance, where the impression fostered by the performance is knowingly contradicted as a matter of course' (1959: 114). The key phrase here is 'relative to a given performance', for although a distinction is drawn between front and backstage, they can in fact be the same place. The definition of the region is fluid, and frontstage can change into backstage and back again in a matter of moments.

There are three main settings: the clerks' room, the environs of the courts, and the pubs near courts and Inns. Settings of minor importance exist, such as the homes of the clerks and barristers, and sporting environments. The clerks' room, however, is the most important of the settings, for it is here that clerk and barrister interact most frequently.

11   Women barristers are addressed as 'Miss', 'Miss Blank' or 'Mrs Blank' (but never 'Mrs' alone), as the situation demands. The appellation 'Madam' is often reserved for lay people.

12   While I was in this particular set of chambers I did some clerking, such as making the afternoon tea for the clerks' room when the 'boy' was attending the courts. On one occasion I was reluctantly forced to apply the last-mentioned rule, 'Do not use the kitchen', and evict a pupil barrister, otherwise the clerks' afternoon tea would have been delayed.

13   The clerk subsequently admitted, 'The fee is under par for the work involved, but I'll make it up on the brief fee.' Both the solicitor and taxing master are more amenable to allowing higher fees on the brief than on the drafting of opinions and other paperwork.

14   Within the Bar a set of chambers is usually referred to by the head of chambers' name, as though it were a trade mark.

15   To have taken up criminal law would have prevented him from having sufficient time to devote to landlord and tenant law.

16   The contradiction outlined here really applies only to crime/common law chambers. Tax, Chancery and other specialities tend to require a long probationary period of the barrister in order to build up and maintain a practice.

17   (1) See Benson (1979: I, ch. 35; II, s. 15). (2) Consider also the following exchanges between Mr D. Seligman, a commissioner, and Mr E. Cooper and Mr C. B. Harrison, two officers of the Barristers' Clerks' Association, during oral testimony given to the Royal Commission on Legal Services on 13 July 1978, at pp. 25–6:

Mr Seligman. Can I come on to another aspect of discrimination. Would you agree with the statement that there is discrimination against women in chambers by clerk and by solicitors, briefing women?

Mr Cooper. Yes, but not in all such chambers, because I have two lady barristers myself, and they are both very good barristers in their own way. We all get on very well, and there is absolutely no discrimination. I have had many lady pupils over the years, and there is no discrimination, either by me or the barristers. But I have found some solicitors—and this applies to other things besides what sex they are—where the solicitor will say, 'Look, on this case, Eric, if you do not mind I would rather not have Miss X,' but I think they are perfectly entitled to say it, just the same as if they wanted to they would say, 'I do not want Bill Bloggs,' because they do not think he is the right person for that type of case.

Mr Seligman. And not discrimination on the grounds that she is a woman?

Mr Cooper. I do not think so, but I cannot say that, because it could be, and certainly there are some such chambers, I think, who in the past at any rate have said, 'We do not have women in chambers'.

Mr Harrison. I think they are going now, are they not?

Mr Cooper. I think they are.

Mr Harrison. We have had two women in chambers for the last twenty years. I think there is very little prejudice.

Mr Seligman. You have the statutory two women, have you, or one woman?

Mr Harrison. No, it's an unfortunate way of putting it, the statutory two women. It just so happens that there have been two women. Could I put it another way? It is not us or the profession that has anything against women or overseas coloured barristers or any other supposed minority. It is the public at large. Because whereas some people will ring me up and they will say, 'Who can do this ouster summons at the Bromley county court tomorrow?' I will say, 'I have got Mrs So-and-so, and I have got Mr . . .'—I will give them a selection—'all of whom work in this,' and they say, 'I will have Mr So-and-so, the clients did not want a woman.' That is not any prejudice on my part, and, frankly, it is no prejudice on the solicitor's part, but the lay client has got a prejudice, much the same as many lay clients have prejudices over colours of skin or racial origins. You can lean over backwards and try and over-compensate, as indeed my chambers nearly did on one occasion when we had an application from a coloured girl to join us. The chambers meeting nearly fell over backwards to say, 'We have got to have her,' more or less on the law basis of 'Let us have the statutory coloured female,' but it was not until I pointed out, 'What are you judging her on, the colour of her skin, on her sex, or her ability? So now let us forget about those elements and let us discuss what her ability is.' She did not match up and so she was not taken on. Some people would probably write to the newspapers very lengthy and learned articles saying it was prejudice on the grounds of colour and sex. It was not that at all, she did not match up to it. (3) See Sachs and Wilson (1978) and Kennedy (1978).

18 A young female barrister, about to enter pupilage, once expressed the fear that in order to obtain a tenancy she would have to sleep with the senior clerk. However, the 'casting–couch' philosophy appears not to have spread to the Temple yet.

19 The members of chambers *instructed* the clerk to refer work to this barrister.

20 A barrister who has the services of a clerk but is assigned no office space in the chambers. Door tenancies are sometimes denoted by the barrister's name being written in letters smaller than those of the tenants proper on the chambers door. See *The Times,* 18 August 1975: 2; Benson (1979: I, para. 33.21).

21 The prejudice at the Bar has resulted in the formation of sets of chambers composed of one nationality or ethnic group, e.g. Greek, black, Indian and so forth. As may be expected, such 'ghetto chambers' tend to be patronised by members of the respective ethnic groups. See Benson (1979: I, ch. 35).

22 The turnover of court work in common law chambers is more rapid than that in civil and Chancery chambers, and therefore barristers in common law sets frequently receive new cases whilst 'on the road'.

23 This clerk qualified his statement by saying that the Bar examinations were not a good indicator of academic brilliance, because the scripts were marked by practising barristers who had little time to devote to their marking.

24 The type of work offered to the barrister and the particular solicitors who send it are also relevant.

25 One clerk stated that he had enough marital problems of his own without attempting to solve those of his governors.

26 At one stage 'neutral' members of chambers were interceding on behalf of the clerk and objectors, attempting to effect a compromise.

27 On being telephoned by the other clerk who was having to clerk this barrister, he informed him exactly how bad the barrister was and sympathised with the other's plight. The other clerk was unable to refuse, because the head of chambers had sanctioned the admittance of the new member.

28 The clerk's bill, however, is always submitted punctually.
29 The relationship between Norman Birkett and his clerk, A. E. Bowker, shows best the level of trust that can develop. See Bowker (1947) and Hyde (1964).

Chapter 4

SOURCES OF WORK AND RELATIONS WITH SOLICITORS

Barristers' work is provided by solicitors. There are exceptions;[1] nevertheless Boulton (1975: 8) says, 'The general rule is that barristers do not see or advise clients or accept briefs or appear as advocates on behalf of clients *without the intervention of a solicitor*' (my emphasis). But the solicitor does not conduct his business with the barrister direct; the solicitor must deal with the clerk. And in fact all communication between barrister and solicitor passes through him. The clerk is the mediator, or, following Boissevain (1974), he can be described as a broker whose job is to bring the right barrister into contact with the solicitor.

Boissevain (1974: 198) characterises a broker as 'a professional manipulator of people and information who brings about communication for profit'. The clerk has many roles *vis-à-vis* the solicitor: he provides counsel, negotiates fees, transmits messages, monitors the progress of cases in the different court lists and acts as a referral service. The profit is the clerk's percentage commission of the fee. Clerks believe their commission comes from two sources, the solicitor (or client) and the barrister. The Barristers' Clerks' Association has used this belief to argue that when a clerk does business with a solicitor he is not acting solely for the benefit of the barrister but is really in the position of agent and broker: that is, he has some degree of autonomy.[2] In addition to the immediate cash reward the clerk can build up 'lines of credit' for favours done which he can call on from solicitors and barristers in the future.

SOURCES OF WORK

Barristers receive their work from diverse sources, but the form is constant—instructions to counsel. A typical brief is a bundle of paper, varying in size with the complexity of the case, tied with a

length of pink tape.[3] The back sheet carries the name of the parties to
the dispute, the court in which the action has been put down to be
heard, the task or set of tasks the solicitor is requesting of counsel,
the name of counsel and of the solicitors. One item often omitted
from the brief is the fee. Most clerks do not like to fix a fee without
first 'perusing the papers', so it is usually marked on the brief in
chambers. An exception to this rule is made in simple cases, e.g.
undefended divorces, when the fee is marked on the brief before it is
sent to the chambers. The fee is frequently composed of two parts;
e.g. an undefended divorce brief might be marked as £10 and £2. The
larger sum covers the court appearances, and the smaller is payment
for a conference between counsel and client, whether or not it is
held.[4]

The largest group providing business for barristers is solicitors:
the next largest, solicitors' clerks.[5] Although solicitors' clerks
generally work in solicitors' offices and perhaps therefore might not
be considered a separate entity, in fact they are a discrete body of
legal personnel who, in large part, organise their own work.[6] It is
one of the jobs of the barrister's clerk to know how to deal with each
of these groups.

Barristers' clerks are frequently on first-name terms with
solicitors, but even so the difference in status is marked. There is
less formality with criminal law than with civil law solicitors.
Furthermore the rank of the barrister's clerk is important in these
relations. A junior clerk describing his initiation into the Temple ten
years earlier remembered the rules laid down by his first senior:
'When I call someone by their first name, you call them Mr
So-and-so; when I call someone Mr So-and-so, you call them Sir;
when I call someone Sir, you don't speak to them.'

There are, however, no discernible status differences between
barristers' clerks and solicitors' clerks. Until some years ago
considerable quantitites of legal work coming out of solicitors'
offices were channelled through solicitors' clerks.[7] A senior clerk
described how business was done. 'All the pubs in Fleet Street—the
George, the Cock, etc.—used to be full of clerks and solicitors'
managing clerks. That was where all the touting was done. The
solicitors' clerks would get boozed on the barrister's clerk and the
work would come in. That type of touting has died out now; there
are no longer those types of solicitors' clerks around.' Even today the
level of interaction between solicitors' and barristers' clerks is high.

They still drink together; they share common backgrounds, and their conversation is less constrained than that between barrister's clerk and solicitor. Barristers' clerks even take solicitors' clerks to the BCA annual dinner.

Most of the remaining sources of business are not as important as solicitors, either in number or in the quantity of work they produce. But there are two exceptions: the Director of Public Prosecutions, the DPP, who is the prime source of work for Treasury counsel, and the Crown, which provides work for the junior counsel to the Treasury.[8] Most central government departments have their own standing counsel who act for them on an *ad hoc* basis. Collectively these types of work represent the upper end of the market.

Further down the scale is the prosecution work distributed by the Attorney General's clerk to those barristers who are on the 'DPP's list'. That is, they do the major prosecution work at courts other than the Central Criminal Court. Still further down the scale is the legal work distributed by the Directorates of Legal Services for the military. Finally, there are the prosecution briefs allocated by the local police forces, either through their own solicitors' departments or through firms of solicitors which handle such work for them. (See Abel-Smith and Stevens, 1968: 113.)

The common feature of these last three sources is that they use barristers who must apply (or rather, their clerks apply on their behalf) to be placed on a list of potential recipients. But a position on the list does not guarantee a flow of work. Officially no barrister can apply to be put on the list. Nevertheless the only way in which a barrister will get 'appointed' is through substantial lobbying by his clerk, so the process is equivalent to making an application. One clerk who had Treasury counsel and barristers on the DPP's list characterised the process this way. 'It's done by suggestion. When a vacancy arises and I think I've got a governor who's right for the job, I have a word with people in the Met [Metropolitan Police] and the DPP's office and any of my governors who are Treasury counsel and on the DPP's list. Then word should get round to the Attorney General.' Another clerk with barristers on the south-eastern circuit said, 'Everyone wants to get on the DPP's list, but this circuit's got too many barristers and not enough work.'

The Director of Public Prosecutions' list is made up and administered by the Attorney General's clerk. There is a separate list for each circuit, and every year the Attorney General's clerk adds to and substracts from the barristers who comprise the three sections of each list.[9] After the list has been drawn up a draft is sent to the leader of the appropriate circuit for his comments, though the Attorney General is not bound to accept his recommendations. It is then the responsibility of the Attorney General's clerk to allocate the prosecution work. A clerk who recently held the post commented that on certain circuits (e.g. the south-eastern) there was rarely sufficient work for the entire list, which has, of course, generated many complaints about the alleged unfairness of the system. The reaction of this same clerk was to dismiss them as 'sour grapes': 'they say it's unfair, especially to those who are not on the list. They say they can do the job better than those who are. And those who are getting work say the quality isn't good enough. Often what we consider the right man for the job is not what the man himself thinks.' But the system is not comprehensive or completely meritocratic. When the Attorney General's clerk has a brief to place he may have a particular barrister in mind, but he faces the same obstacles as any solicitor who briefs a barrister. For example, when one Attorney General's clerk tried to place a brief on a northern circuit, his first choice was unavailable and so were the next five he named. On the seventh attempt he was lucky, but the barrister came from lower down the list than he wanted.

Clerks frequently complain among themselves about the inequities of the system, the main grumble being that the Attorney General's clerk keeps the most lucrative briefs for his own chambers.[10] But no clerk has ever pressed the point, for fear of losing prosecution work. Hence the system, unless subjected to pressure for reform, is likely to continue as the personal fief of the Attorney General's clerk.[11]

The police prosecution lists, although more openly competitive than the DPP's list, are overmanned and underworked. The most important list in London is the 'SMP list', that of the Solicitor for the Metropolitan Police. The work consists mainly of small cases, but they can be profitable if there are enough of them. Unfortunately for the barristers who specialise in SMP list work, they are subject to periodic raids by other barristers when other types of work are scarce. One senior clerk whose chambers took in substantial quantities of SMP prosecution work complained that 'a lot of civil barristers, just starting out, like to do prosecution work, and when their civil practices build up they drop it'. He felt that only barristers seriously committed to prosecution work should get the briefs.[12] All police prosecution lists are subject to closure when the solicitor's department considers the current stock of counsel sufficient to meet demand. A clerk who was trying to launch a new set of chambers encountered the overmanning problem when he tried to get his barristers on the SMP list: there was a waiting list of two hundred. On occasion the number has been as high as a thousand, resulting in an effective wait of two or three years.

The SMP is staffed by a mixture of admitted and unadmitted personnel, who distribute the briefs to those on the list. It is the unadmitted staff who are closest to the clerks. Their ranks are largely composed of retired policemen. They meet them socially and usually attend the annual football match between Lincoln's Inn and Temple clerks. But the move towards professionalisation in the SMP—the greater use of admitted staff—is weakening these traditional links. Even so, contacts at the SMP are still cultivated in the hope of influencing the distribution of prosecution briefs.

But the solicitor surpasses in importance all these sources of work. How does the barrister's clerk shape his relationship with the solicitor?

TOUTING

In the broadest sense of the word, clerks tout all their clients. It is a grey area in which the Bar has been concerned only to delineate broad principles.[13] However, touting varies in degrees of perceived wickedness, and clerks must learn which are permissible and which are not. Moreover they can only develop the skill on a case-by-case basis: each solicitor requires a different approach. The ultimate goal of the barrister's clerk is to establish a stable group of 'chambers solicitors', who rely mainly on one or two sets of chambers for their counsel. While the large, well established chambers have succeeded in building their groups of solicitors, the lesser ones must compete among themselves for business. And, of course, many solicitors know this.

When a solicitor calls a barrister's clerk to retain a barrister, he expects and requires, quite simply, three things: the 'right' barrister at the 'right' price at the 'right' time. If a clerk can meet all three requirements he has gone a long way towards cultivating a chambers solicitor. Frequently he has to appeal to his network of colleagues to help resolve the omnipresent problem of satisfying the solicitor.

Conversely the clerk expects the solicitor to send all the work he can to his chambers, not quibble over fees and pay them regularly, not be unduly demanding of his time, and understand when he substitutes a different barrister at the last moment. If, however, the solicitor's and the clerk's expectations are compared they appear almost irreconcilable. It is for the clerk to provide the solution: the solicitor can always transfer his business elsewhere.

Some of the newer sets of chambers attempt to generate a supply of briefs by joining the 'return circuit', taking work transferred from other chambers.[14] Returns are rarely sufficient to sustain a set of chambers; the clerk must attract briefs from more direct sources. He may be lucky, like the young senior who found his first chambers solicitor by getting him a barrister in court at short notice. From that time on he received most of the solicitor's litigation work. Or the clerk may have to push himself into the legal community. One, on opening a new set of chambers, spent over a hundred pounds the first week entertaining potential clients. He had gained an entry into the local community through the help of a solicitor with whom he had done a good deal of business. To round off the week he held a small reception to introduce his barristers to the local solicitors. Most of them came, but half of them felt he had overstepped the line into illicit touting[15] and refused to brief the chambers. Among them were the solicitor who distributed the prosecution briefs and one of the largest firms in the area, so that the gamble paid off only in part.

Most barristers' clerks are dissatisfied with the number of solicitors who brief their chambers. A growing clientele enables the chambers to expand. In the clerk's view, moreover, the quality of firms of solicitors is always open to improvement. One observed, 'what I want is the *quantity* of work, then I can take the *quality* from that.' Another, who was trying to expand his commercial law chambers, explained that half their work came from City solicitors and half from the provinces.[16] 'I want regular work from the big ten firms in the City. There are some chambers that get sufficient work from one or two of these. While we may get one or two briefs a year from a country solicitor, the City firms could send down twenty in a day. It's difficult getting work from these firms, but it should come in time.'

As the clerk thinks he is approaching the optimal number of solicitors he will try to sift out the better-quality firms. A clerk whose chambers had thrived on the growth of neighbourhood law centre work was able to pass it on to others as he began to attract more remunerative briefs from elsewhere. Although he was reducing his reliance on the neighbourhood law centres, they still sent him their serious cases.

This winnowing, or graduating, process often prompts a change in the clerk's attitude towards solicitors and clients. A kind of snobbery intrudes. For example, a junior clerk to a civil law set emphasised the service aspect of the clerk's role. So when a Midland firm of solicitors called to ask for the name of a 'good' firm of London solicitors he expected both firms to remember him in the future. The same man was not so obliging when another solicitor requested a barrister to do a child-stealing case. The clerk was extremely blunt. He told the solicitor that his chambers dealt only in commercial, not criminal law, and refused to recommend another set. Another clerk refused to accept work from solicitors who caused him 'aggro' (trouble). In one instance a solicitor who had been sending small amounts of work yet demanded fee notes and wrote what the clerk considered offensive letters was told to take his work elsewhere and referred to a smaller set. A solicitor at a neighbourhood law centre who had used these chambers extensively found himself shunted aside. When he telephoned, the junior clerk would tell him, on the senior's instructions, that 'if he would care to leave his number we'll call back as soon as possible'. He was annoyed—'He knows my bloody number backwards'—but there was little he could do but wait. In sum, this sifting of the solicitors effectively nullifies the impact of the cab-rank rule of the Bar.[17]

Doing favours—the service aspect of the clerk's job—is the greatest investment the clerk is called on to make when trying to capture a solicitor. It can be extreme. One clerk remembered a solicitor who would telephone him at 3 a.m. to find a barrister for the morning—'I always did, too.' And failure can be costly. A clerk had to drive to the north of England from London to explain himself after failing to provide two Queen's Counsel. Fortunately he was able to find acceptable substitutes, and he took the solicitors out to dinner. Another had to send a barrister to Wales, entailing an overnight stay, to attend a five-minute county court hearing because the solicitors wanted to stay the proceedings. Not only was the fee negligible but the clerk lost the use of a barrister for a day.

Describing his attitude towards solicitors, a civil law clerk said,

'The key word is integrity; the Bar has it, and so have the clerks. Now some City firms of solicitors are good, and so is one on the western circuit, but the rest are hopeless. We still try and do our best for them. Sure, you could screw a client, but next time he wouldn't come back. Or somebody asks me for a bankruptcy expert and I'll say, "Well, you're better off if you go to No. X, Paper Buildings, they've got the experts." So the solicitor will think, "There's a man who knows what it's all about." and he'll come back to me. It's not worth winning the battle to lose the war.'

The largest category of favours concerns fee-cutting, including waiving the fee. It is a sensitive matter between clerk and solicitor, because each believes the other is motivated by self-interest. The clerk considers a reduced fee as a concession that must be recouped in the future. Most clerks, when encouraging work from a solicitor, will readily reduce fees by small, even large, amounts if the solicitor asks. One clerk halved a fee in a divorce matter at the solicitor's request because the lay client had no money. Yet the clerks sometimes resent it when they believe there is no justification for a reduction. In a case involving a claim of £100,000 the solicitor suggested a fee of £100. The clerk felt £250 was more realistic. They compromised on £160. But the clerk said, 'He's trying it on, he just wants it for his own pocket. I mean, he's getting somewhere near a thousand quid for this.' Another solicitor wrote to a clerk asking for a reduction in a counsel's fee that had been outstanding for six years, because of the delay in payment. The clerk was furious.

A potentially contentious matter between barristers' clerks and solicitors is the referral of briefs to barristers in the same chambers or to other chambers. This is the 'return circuit'. In common law chambers clerks strongly believe in the interchangeability of barristers. The frenetic pace of activity in the clerks' room creates a 'battery farm' atmosphere which tends to dehumanise the clients' cases. Most clerks hold the view that nearly all small and medium-sized briefs could be handled competently by any barrister. When last-minute changes of counsel have to be made the clerk hopes the solicitor will understand and accept the situation. Cases involving legally aided clients are most subject to this treatment. A criminal law clerk explained that list officers, especially at the Old Bailey, were more sympathetic to privately financed clients, and that a legally aided client should consider himself lucky to get any barrister. The clerk agreed: it made the planning of his diary very easy.

Occasionally a clerk returns or refers a brief for reasons other than lack of suitable counsel. For example, a solicitor requiring an opinion on a problem of Asian family law contacted the clerk of a chambers where the head of the set used to be an expert in this field. The clerk warned him he should find another barrister. 'Mr X. is one of the most senior silks at the Bar, he doesn't do this type of case. He used to work in the Far East and, of course, joined the Bar out there. But now he spends all his time on big trials. Look, the client will be *dead* by the time he does this opinion.' For, as the clerk argued, 'Mr X. will take this case and then nine months later the solicitors will phone up and say where is it? He's like that. He would do it eventually but he would make the clerk's life a misery—dictating to the typist, trying to find books. It would probably take a week and cost £500 in time. Obviously they just looked through the Law List.' The brief nevertheless arrived, to the clerk's annoyance. He sent it to another chambers and afterwards rang the solicitor to tell him where it had gone.

When touting solicitors and solicitors' clerks, the barrister's clerk must avoid losing his temper if provoked. He must never lose face, otherwise he may lose the client. One clerk, who forbade smoking in his clerks' room, had to suppress his outrage at a solicitor who, whenever he came to the chambers, would put his feet up on the senior's desk and smoke a pipe. Whatever the provocation, the clerk has to control himself. A group of clerks were entertaining a solicitor's clerk in a pub when he began to get abusive about barristers' clerks and barristers, accusing them of being 'crooks' and 'taking the lay clients for a ride'. Although one of the group was having difficulty containing himself, the others went on plying the man with beer, until he was too drunk to talk. Another solicitor's clerk told a barrister's clerk that those who supplied the work 'owned' the barrister, and therefore everyone should 'jump' at the solicitor's word. The clerk could only reply that a small volume of work gave proportionately small rights in the barrister.

Although clerks can be annoyed by solicitors and their clerks, they are impotent to affect their behaviour. A clerk to a revenue law set of chambers, where most of the lawyers' business was conducted in chambers conferences, felt one of his senior barristers had been insulted when a solicitor failed to turn up for a conference which had been booked three weeks before. The solicitor had been expecting a telephone call from the United States. As the clerk put it, 'Why couldn't he get his call transferred here? After all, it's *only* Mr Z., QC!'

Occasionally clerks find themselves having to protect the solicitor or his clerk, especially from barristers who are trying to collect overdue fees. One had to arrange for his head of chambers to defend a solicitor's clerk against a charge of intimidating witnesses. The solicitor's clerk was too valuable a supplier of work to lose.

Despite the fact that barristers' clerks engage in practices which they call touting and yet regard as normal, it does not prevent them from deprecating what they believe to be 'real' touting. A common law clerk analysed the problem thus: 'Looking after your own is all right, but *touting* is wrong. It means you're going round taking work away from other clerks. And it's something you wouldn't want to happen to yourself.'

A further problem arises when a set of chambers splits up: who 'owns' the chambers' solicitors? One clerk said, 'Well, that's different from straight touting: you're entitled to take work from old to new chambers.' A junior clerk who became senior to a small segment of a split set reported that no chambers solicitors had followed him, only those who instructed certain barristers; the others had preferred to remain with the larger segment. A former chairman of the BCA said that clerks should follow the etiquette of the Bar in regard to touting. He even went on to suggest that a clerk should not find any work for a barrister.[18] To most clerks this is an extreme opinion, one that is given scant credence. But as a clerk establishes his chambers and his stock of solicitors his outlook on touting may begin to narrow somewhat. And as chambers are tending to increase in size the need for explicit touting is diminishing. The entrepreneurial role of the clerk gives way to that of an administrator.[19] In some ways, then, touting is beginning to be driven 'underground'. For example, a clerk who was setting up a new set of chambers, eager for prosecution work, was helped by a court official to entertain a clerk from a police prosecution department. The hospitality was lavish: drinks, dinner in Mayfair and a strip club to finish. Total cost of the evening, some £200. The barrister's clerk took very careful precautions not to be seen in or near the Temple with his party in case tongues wagged.

SALESMANSHIP

Ideally a clerk should never allow a solicitor to place a brief with
another set of chambers except for functional reasons such as a lack
of appropriate expertise in his own. He has to be a master of the art of
persuading solicitors that the next-best alternative is just as good.
When a common law clerk was unable to provide a junior counsel of
some seniority he managed to persuade the solicitor to accept an
alternative who was available. 'He's a strong cross-examiner, a good
lawyer. Does most of his work in the Crown Court, you
know—difficult drug cases. He was in the R—— enquiry, junior to
Mr X., and junior to Mr S. in the W—— enquiry.' In a similar
situation a civil law clerk persuaded a solicitor to try a barrister he
had never used before. 'He's a very able man, sir, very conscientious.
He was a pupil here a couple of years ago—you remember him,
blond hair, glasses . . . that's right . . . Oh, yes, sir, he studies the
papers well beforehand, and by the time the case comes round he
knows all about it. I can certainly recommend him, sir.' Sometimes,
if a particularly lucrative case is sent in for a barrister who is
otherwise booked, the clerk will shift the original case to someone of
lesser standing.

Certain clients specify which counsel they will use from a list.
The DPP's list is a case in point. If the clerk cannot provide a name
from the list it is virtually impossible to sell another who is not on it.
Other lists are less rigid; for example, the list of counsel drawn up by
the insurance companies. Here a clerk may be able to persuade the
company to try an unlisted man, who may, as a result, end up
joining the list.

The selling or substitution of barristers has to be combined with
the aim of providing the most suitable barrister for the client. As one
clerk put it, 'It's a matter of horses for courses. Do you want a
fighter, or what?' In commenting on the solicitor's need for the right
barrister (a QC for a plea of mitigation at a Crown court), the clerk
said, 'This case needs the soft touch, a velvet approach, whereas
somebody like Mr X., QC, is a drum-beater, the type you need for
bomb trials. You've got to consider the judge, and this ones's an
establishment figure.' The 'most suitable' barrister must also accord
with the prejudices of the solicitor. A clerk who was trying to find a
barrister for a client offered the choice of a woman in practice or a
male pupil. The solicitor preferred the pupil, even though both he

and the clerk knew the woman was the better lawyer.

FIXING AND COLLECTING FEES

Critics of the barrister's clerk (see Zander, 1968; Abel-Smith and
Stevens, 1968) argue that his prime concern is to set each fee as high
as possible, for his own benefit. I think I have shown that the general
tenor of the clerk's relations with his suppliers is not like that.
Indeed, his most important concern is to regulate fees so as to
maintain a consistent flow of work. In the area of criminal law, the
fixing of fees by the clerk is in decline. These fees, mostly legal aid,
are settled by the taxing officers of the Crown courts on the basis of
the information provided on the 'pink form'.[20] In civil actions, and
in non-legally-aided criminal proceedings, the fee should be
negotiated before the trial (following the general rule; see Boulton,
1975: 48–52). Paperwork fees are agreed after the work has been
done, and many are now standardised.

Before settling a fee the clerk likes to see the brief to evaluate its
complexity and the time needed for preparation. No one wants to
decide a fee on an unseen brief. One clerk said that some solicitors
'tried it on' by describing a case as minor, then sending in a hefty
brief after the fee had been agreed. For example, one solicitor needed
a junior barrister for a plea of mitigation—normally a
straightforward matter; the papers, however, numbered over four
hundred pages, which meant increasing considerably the 'perusing
the papers' element of the fee.

In negotiations between clerk and solicitor the clerk usually
proposes a fee, which the solicitor may accept or not. Most clerks
agreed that solicitors generally accepted their proposals, only
seeking modifications for poor clients. The fee consists mainly of the
following expenses: the amount of time spent on drafting and
preparation, or the time that should have been spent (a barrister may
be fast or slow); the size of the claim; the seniority of the barrister;
and a notion of a crude hourly rate for each barrister.[21] The central
criterion in evaluating the fee is 'experience'. One criminal law clerk
went so far as to say that there ought to be *two* fees for criminal work,
one for 'advocacy', the other for 'law'. The idiosyncrasies of
solicitors are also taken into account: a solicitor who quibbled over
every fee quoted to him was always charged slightly more to
allow for the inevitable haggling. Most clerks increase the barrister's

fees as a way of attenuating the supply of work when a barrister is becoming dangerously overloaded. One clerk, for example, quoted £200 for an appearance in a magistrate's court. He never expected to get the brief: the exaggerated fee was a message to the solicitor to look elsewhere. But the major fees, such as those required for Queen's Counsel, are subject to extensive negotiation between clerk and solicitor. And where several QCs are involved in a single case the clerks will discuss between themselves what they consider the appropriate level of fees before they negotiate with the solicitors.

After completion of a barrister's work the brief, opinion or pleadings are returned to the solicitor with a fee note. (See over.) At the bottom of most fee notes is a space for the date when the fee note has been resubmitted. The process of collecting fees is not a simple task; it requires tact and restraint. Nearly all clerks have difficulty in obtaining fees from solicitors, including the legal aid authorities. Even though reminders are sent, the effect is small; the six-year-old fee mentioned above is an example.

Barrister's clerks accept that many solicitors' litigation departments are understaffed and overworked.[22] But the root of the problem does not lie only with the solicitors. In chambers with a small staff little time is spared for fee collecting, and that at irregular intervals. Larger chambers have reduced the problem by employing accounts staff to cope with fees. Clerks who adopted this system felt the pay-off in increased efficiency (and cash flow) justified the expense.[23] It has not completely resolved the problem of overdue payments, however. Even discussions between the Bar and the Law Society have failed to do so.

One fear is that constantly pestering clients for payment could result in their business moving to other chambers. So some clerks feel they have to shield their solicitors from the actions of impetuous barristers. For example, a barrister wrote to a solicitor threatening to report him to the Law Society for non-payment. The letter was to be sent under the clerk's name, but he held it back until the barrister forgot about it: he did not want to upset the solicitor. It is better to have work and slow payment than no work at all.

The worst offenders are found among the smaller, less successful firms who tend to rely on the smaller and newer chambers. At the opposite end of the scale, the clerk of a heavily briefed specialist set said there was no backlog of fees in his chambers; the solicitors always paid regularly.

Tax invoice No. ....   12 Fountain Court
Telephone: 021-353 1234   Temple, EC4 1QS

Solicitor's ref:

Messrs Woodcock and Woodcock

— — — — — — — — — — — —

Fees of

Mr J. Cade

VAT Registration No. 243 7368 64

Legal Aid No. ....

			TAX POINT:	
	Re: *Lancashire Assurance Co. Ltd* v. *Yorkshire Properties Ltd*			
1975				
11 Nov.	Settling defence		£15.00	£1.20
11 Nov.	Advice		£20.00	£1.60
8 Dec.	Brief appellant			
8 Dec.	Conference (Judge in Chambers — 16.12.75)		£25.00	£2.00
12 Dec.	Advise in conference		£10.00	£0.80
22 Dec.	Settling defence		£10.00	£0.80
1976				
12 Mar.	Brief defendant			
12 Mar.	Conference (Mayor's and City of London Court)		£60.00	£4.80
30 Mar.	Brief on adjourned hearing		£25.00	£2.00
			£165.00	£13.20
	VALID ONLY WHEN RECEIPTED			
Fee note rendered	5 Apr.	10 June	20 Aug.	

A typical fee note

Generally clerks expect and live with the delay between 'rendering the fee note' and actual payment.[24] One clerk had several hundred unpaid fees spanning the previous ten years. In many cases a wait of two to three years was considered normal. And it is those barristers who are starting their career who are the most affected. Clerks tend to be less than zealous in collecting fees for their neophytes.[25] These barristers are the least remunerative and most expendable, for no clerk wants to endanger the supply of work for the sake of a few beginners. Thus one clerk, before admitting a new barrister to his chambers, verified first that he had sufficient funds to support himself for two years.

The legal aid authorities do not make the collection process any easier. Whereas the Crown courts pay solicitors and barristers direct, magistrates' courts send the fees to the solicitors, who are supposed to pass on the barrister's portion. This too works mainly against the novice. Such fees are usually small, and though a clerk can appeal against a taxation, most thought the small amounts involved did not warrant the 'aggravation' when their time could be more profitably spent on other tasks. But as one clerk noted, 'Sometimes the amounts are so small it's not worth the bother to appeal, but over time it all mounts up.'

The ultimate sanction against non-payment is to report the solicitor to the Law Society and claim on the compensation fund.[26] The efficacy of this tactic depends, however, on the solicitor having received payment from the lay client, which the majority of clerks agreed was difficult if not impossible to prove. One clerk cited several solicitors' reactions when a QC of his was appointed to the Bench; after asking for settlement of the unpaid fees, the solicitor told him, 'You can't prove the client's paid me, therefore I'm not going to pay.' Another clerk tried to extract some unpaid fees from a former solicitor who had been struck off the roll. Over a long period he had sought payment, without success. Finally he rang the ex-solicitor and warned him that unless payment was settled immediately he would report him to the Law Society. The clerk did not expect to get the fees, but a report to the Law Society would at least make it more difficult for the ex-solicitor to be reinstated.

In conclusion, the fragmented and individualistic nature of the Bar increases the improbability of clerks ever being able to take concerted action against solicitors who default on payment. By contrast, the Victoria Bar in Australia has, in the past, been able to

use blacklisting tactics, on behalf of the younger members of the
Bar, against defaulting solicitors. But the Victoria Bar is more
cohesive than the English one.[27] In England an attempt to operate
a similar blacklist, by the Chancery Clerks' Association, failed
through lack of support.

CONCLUSION

The main goal of the barrister's clerk is to build up a stock of
solicitors for his chambers. He expects to get most, if not all, of the
work of those solicitors. And clerks get upset if they see a solicitor
use other chambers. One clerk was annoyed when he discovered, by
looking through the cases at a list office, that one of his main
solicitors had briefed another chambers. 'I went down to the Old
Bailey, and there was a card there with Mrs X. leading Mr Y.:
attempted murder; A., B. and C. the solicitors. Bloody cheek.' In
the pursuit of his goal the clerk provides extra services for the
solicitors—referrals, allowing them to use chambers facilities. In
time a close relationship is built up. As one clerk put it, 'It's *very*
important to build up a good relationship with the solicitor. It takes
months or even longer. It's done through mutual respect, obligation
and trust.' In effect the clerk touts the solicitor.

The barrister's clerk is the nexus of the litigation system for the
solicitor. By virtue of his brokerage activities he manipulates the
system to the advantage of his professional client. The more
extensive and highly connected are the networks of the clerk, the
greater his appeal to the solicitor. As the chambers progress, the
clerk can become selective about the solicitors for whom he chooses
to work.

Though this is advantageous for the clerk, it does nullify the effect
of the cab-rank rule. The existence of the rule has been the
foundation from which the Bar argues whenever it is under attack,
especially the rights of audience the Bar holds. The rule is
substantially a myth.[28] The reality is that the clerk can and does select
the work for the barrister according to how it benefits the chambers.
The Royal Commission on Legal Services accepted the myth
without examining it thoroughly. Perhaps the cab-rank rule should
be renamed the 'limousine-for-hire rule'.

When the chambers' stock of solicitors is complete, much of the creative, entrepreneurial work of the clerk disappears and the administrative aspect of his job moves into the ascendancy.

NOTES

1 See Benson (1979: I, 222):
'Restrictions on direct access to counsel
19.2 A barrister may accept professional work (whether for a fee or not) only if instructed by a solicitor, except where he has instructions from:

   (1) a patent agent in respect of non-contentious matters relating to patents, trade marks and designs or in respect of hearings before certain tribunals;
   (b) a parliamentary agent, in respect of draft bills or amendments to bills;
   (c) a clerk to a local authority in respect of non-contentious business or to appear at a local inquiry;
   (d) the Chief Land Registrar, to advise on titles;
   (e) the Secretary of the Church Assembly to draft Church Assembly Measures, amendments thereto or rules thereunder;
   (f) a lay client, in order to examine for libel and contempt material which is to be published;
   (g) a foreign lawyer, if no United Kingdom litigation or arbitration has been instituted and the instructions do not involve work in the United Kingdom of a character which is customarily associated with solicitors;
   (h) a lay client who is not resident in the United Kingdom, in respect of a matter 'essentially arising outside the United Kingdom';
   (j) a prisoner in the dock in the Crown Court.'

2 The BCA has argued that a clerk's fee is a combination of payments from principal and solicitor, hence the semblance of autonomy.
3 Most solicitors use pink tape. Prosecution briefs are tied together with white tape. Central and local government briefs are tied with green tape. None of these colours is compulsory, but custom prevails. Instructions to counsel contain, in theory, the necessary and sufficient information for a barrister to argue a case or write an opinion or draft documents. The materials might consist of interviews with witnesses, photographs, plans, etc.
4 Boulton (1975: 50, 52) states: 'Save in a few well recognised and exceptional cases, such as appearing for a Public Department or for the Police in criminal prosecutions, or for an assisted person under the Legal Aid and Advice Act 1959, a barrister should not appear in Court upon a brief which has no fee marked on it.'
5 The nomenclature is unimportant here. I use the term 'solicitor's clerk' rather than 'legal executive' because the image evoked has greater descriptive power over the range of unadmitted personnel operating in this area.
6 Zander (1978: 299–302).

7 Even now litigation is in large part handled by solicitors' clerks in large as well as small firms.

8 Treasury counsel are the counsel to the Crown at the Central Criminal Court. They are a group of barristers appointed by the Attorney General to prosecute the most serious cases. Junior counsel to the Treasury undertake civil work for the Crown. There are two of them: one in the Queen's Bench Division and one in the Chancery Division of the High Court. See Abel-Smith and Stevens (1968: 112–13).

9 Barristers are assigned to a section of the list according to the weight of case they are able to handle.

10 See chapter 3.

11 In *The Law Officers of the Crown* Edwards (1964) provides no details of the Attorney General's patronage. Cf. Simon (1965) and *The Law Times,* 15 March 1957: 137–8, and see Caplan (1978: 135).

12 This is an instance of the principle of the cab-rank rule of the Bar being flouted.

13 Boulton (1975: 55–7) lays down only 'statements of principle'. Cf. *Code of Professional Responsibility* of the American Bar Association (adopted 1970, amended 1970, 1974, 1975 and 1977), Canon 2, especially D.R.2–101 Publicity. And see proposed *Model Rules of Professional Conduct* of the ABA Commission on Evaluation of Professional Standards (1980), rule 9.

14 See chapter 6, and cf. Zander (1968: ch. 11) and Benson (1979: I, 300–1).

15 At one point even the barristers became concerned that the clerk might have been overstepping the bounds of propriety.

16 By City firms I mean those that constitute the City of London Solicitors' Company (CLSC). In its memorandum of evidence to the Royal Commission on Legal Services the CLSC outlined its work thus:

(a) Euro-dollar and other foreign currency bank financings and Euro-dollar bond issues.
(b) Maritime law, including marine insurance, admiralty and maritime and commodity arbitrations.
(c) Other overseas commercial work.
(d) EEC work.

17 See, for example, Benson (1979: I, ch. 17).

18 This former chairman of the BCA clerked a very successful set of chambers and could therefore afford to take a hard line. His successors have had similar backgrounds and also held similar views.

19 See chapter 2.

20 The 'pink form' is a case memorandum. It was designed in consultation with the Barristers' Clerks' Association. The form requires information on whether the case was a fight or plea, the number of defendants, the number of witnesses, the number of pages of statements and exhibits, the number of hours spent getting up the case, the time spent in conferences and giving oral opinions, the number of advices written, the number of documents prepared, the number of applications made and practice directions requested, the number of

days spent in court, the number of conferences held during the trial, the amount of time lost during the trial, any special features in the defence (e.g. expert evidence), travelling and hotel expenses. See Benson (1979: I, annex 37.5).

21 See 'The Bar Council scheme for improving the information on which counsel's fees are assessed', *Guardian Gazette,* 26 November 1975: 1177–8; Graham-Green (1973); Benson (1979: I, ch. 37). Years of call are not always an accurate guide, especially for the solicitor, as the date of call does not indicate the time spent in practice, only the date on which the person was admitted to the Bar. Thus one clerk had a barrister who spent seven years as a local authority lawyer before entering private practice. Nevertheless the barrister was called to the Bar at the start of his career as a lawyer, making it easy for the clerk to pass him off as more experienced than was warranted. 'This made it easy for him to get work because of his call, and nobody knew he had had that gap [seven years]. Very handy, that.'

In a lecture to young clerks (Harrison, n.d.) the lecturer said:
'I think it would be as well if I talk about the methods by which fees are set.

Firstly, fees by agreement. How do we assess a fee?

(a) There is the work involved. The hours that it is going to occupy, the thought, the experience of the man concerned, how much paper there is to read.

(b) Where is the work to be done? Clearly, assuming you had a London-based counsel, if it is in London chambers, or in London at a convenient place, it would be very different if the matter was in Newcastle. Items like fares, hotel and those aspects come into play.

(c) There is the client's ability to pay. A large public company, for example, is in a rather different position from an elderly widow who just falls outside the provisions of the Legal Aid and Advice Act because she happens to have £2,000 cash in the bank. One has got to consider the means of the client.

(d) There is the standing of your principal. His experience, the demand for his services. Put it this way— we can all sing in our bathtub but we we do not command the money for singing in our bathtub that Frank Sinatra commands at the Royal Albert Hall. Why? I am quite certain we can all sing as well as Frank Sinatra. It is a matter of supply and demand. Our principals have a supply and demand element which goes to make up the fee. I have a little slogan that I always use in this regard. I say, 'Let the work shed you.' If the barrister has got so many cases at £50, then do not bother with £25 ones. If I can get £100 cases, we are not going to bother with the £50 ones. Once you start saying 'I am not going to do anything under a certain figure' then you could land up doing very little. You may be a very precious orchid, but who wants a dead orchid!'

22 The following figures are from Benson (1979: II, table 16.58):

Percentages of fee income and fee earners for different categories of work

	No. of firms responding	Total fee income (%)	Fee earners (%)
Conveyancing	879	45·8	37·2
Probate	846	13·9	14·6
Company	655	12·0	6·8
Other non-contentious	697	4·6	8·0
Matrimonial	743	5·6	9·8
Crime	662	4·3	7·3
Personal injury	671	3·5	5·8
Other contentious	764	10·3	10·5
All categories of work		100·0	100·0

23 Some senior clerks paid the salaries of their accounts clerks as their contribution to chambers expenses.
24 See appendix 2 on collecting fees.
25 The issues of slow payment and non-payment of fees generated some articles and correspondence in the *Guardian Gazette* in 1974: 375 (the original article that prompted the correspondence); I. H. Benjamin 'Slow payment of counsel's fees', 22 May 1974: 490; letter, 26 June 1974: 621; letter, 31 July 1974: 752; letter, 25 September 1974: 925; letter, 27 November 1974: 1202; see also *Sunday Times,* 27 March 1977. On reducing the delay in payments of fees by legal aid authorities (criminal) see 'Crown court fees—London area', *Guardian Gazette,* 29 June 1977: 552.
26 See Boulton (1975: 50–1) for procedure on reporting solicitors for non-payment of fees and the recovery of unpaid fees through the Law Society's compensation fund. Before the latter procedures are invoked there is a perliminary procedure designed by the Bar Council (1974) to elicit the fee from the recalcitrant solicitor.
27 I am grateful to Mr John Dwyer of the Victoria Bar for this information.
28 See Reisman (1979: ch. 1) for an analysis of *myth system* and *operational code.*

Chapter 5
SCHEDULING COURT CASES

One of the principal goals of the barrister's clerk is to make the most efficient use of his basic resources, namely his barristers. In achieving this goal the scheduling of court cases is of integral importance. Both solicitors (and other suppliers of work) and barristers depend on the clerk to keep track of the progress of cases through the court lists. From the clerk's point of view, efficient listing means maximum use of his barristers, and being able to inform solicitors of the exact position of their cases in the lists so that they may monitor and adjust the timing and pacing of the cases. (The wishes of the solicitor have high priority with the clerk.)

Each type of court has its own listing procedure; the basic distinction is between civil and criminal jurisdictions. The High Court and Court of Appeal listing procedures are regulated by various orders in *The Supreme Court Practice*.[1] Outside the Supreme Court the remaining civil courts are self-regulating, without regard to any external authority. On the other side, criminal courts were rationalised by the Courts Act, 1971, which followed the Beeching report (1969). Included in the restructuring of the Quarter Sessions and Assizes was a new approach to the scheduling of trials designed to reduce waiting periods.[2]

The actual mechanics of listing, however, are determined between the list officers of the various courts and the barristers' clerks who transact business in those courts.[3] Efficient listing requires the careful exercise of the clerks' interpersonal skills. They must be aware of the preferences and prejudices of the various list officers. In time they build up a relationship of trust and mutual dependence, which has both formal and informal aspects. Up front, clerks must show list officers respect and consideration. Backstage, there are fundamental differences of outlook and attitude between clerks and list officers. These differences are due to the clerk's belief that he upholds free-market, entrepreneurial values, whereas the list officer is an organisation man and represents the bureaucracy—he is just a civil servant. Barristers' clerks use the phrase 'civil servant' as a derogatory term. It embodies the cosy security inherent in the list officer's position (i.e. regular salary, holidays and pension), and the monotony of the regular hours he works. Clerks see these things as symbolic of effeteness. Of course, both list officers and clerks are aware of the difference in outlook, especially as some of the former have been barristers' clerks themselves.[4]

Clerks negotiate listing matters with the officers both face-to-face and by telephone. Daily listing sessions at which the clerk must be present are held at the Law Courts in the Strand and at the Central Criminal Court. The other Crown courts in London hold listing sessions less frequently, and clerks communicate with them mainly by telephone.

The following discussion of the relationships formed between clerks and list officers concentrates on the London courts within the context of civil and criminal jurisdictions.

LISTING: CIVIL LAW

The divisions and courts which make up the Supreme Court all have their own procedures for organising their schedules. Every day the results are published in the *Daily Cause List*. It appears in the form of a newspaper ten to fifteen pages long, which is distributed to the chambers in the Inns during the afternoon. Its preparation is a product of much concentrated activity by clerks and list officers during the day.

The compilation of the various lists—warned jury lists, warned non-jury lists, matrimonial causes, witness and non-witness lists, applications and summonses in chambers, etc.—takes place at a late stage in the litigation process, at the termination of the interlocutory stages. The *Daily Cause List* consists of two main sections. The first shows which cases are currently being tried or about to be tried. Most courts in the High Court and Court of Appeal start at 10.30 a.m. If, however, a court is to hear several matters the cases may be ranked by being classified 'at half-past ten', 'not before half-past 11', 'not before two o'clock', and so on. The second section is composed of the different warned lists out of which the cases for hearing are taken.[5]

Each afternoon, between 1 p.m. and 3 p.m., the clerks whose barristers appear in the Queen's Bench and Family Divisions make a circuit of the list offices in the Law Courts. Generally, this involves one clerk from each set of chambers, usually the senior or first junior but occasionally the second junior is sent.

The first office on the circuit is that of the Clerk of the Rules, where matrimonial causes are arranged. The relationship between clerks and staff in the Clerk of the Rules' office is informal and the atmosphere is relaxed. The clerks start gathering in the corridor outside some time before 1.30 p.m., where they chat and exchange gossip. At 1.30 p.m. the door opens and the clerks rush into the room, which is too small to hold them all. The three list officers sit close to the walls, and even though there is space in the centre of the room for the clerks to stand in they prefer to squeeze into the gaps behind and between the list officers. The arranging of the list resembles the activity on the floor of the stock exchange, where everyone is shouting. As one clerk proposes a date another will voice an objection, and so on, until the list is complete. The nature of the cases here makes the construction of the list a relatively simple matter compared with the complex planning often required in other courts. Nevertheless even when forward planning is necessary the informal style of the Clerk of the Rules' office never varies.

Around 2 p.m. the clerks leave to go to the Queen's Bench Division(QBD) list office. It consists of two small, narrow rooms. One is an ante-room where the clerks wait until called, the other is where the business is conducted. The list officers sit along one of the long walls with the clerks standing in front of them. The atmosphere is more subdued than in the Clerk of the Rules' office. A clerk will position himself at the front or back of the crowd, depending on the number of cases he controls. Some traditionally stand near the front and others occupy particular seats, as in a gentlemen's club. But the main press of the crowd (often over a hundred) throngs around the door between the two rooms.

The procedure too is also more formal than at the Clerk of the Rules': the chief Clerk of the Lists orchestrates the business with a certain amount of solemnity from beginning to end. His list is made up of two parts: dated and undated actions. The former are dated for hearing and as vacancies occur in courts these are assigned first. As the list officer announces which court and judge a case is going to, an associate cuts the name of the case from a sheet and pastes it on to a master plan in front of him. The rate at which he can perform his scissors-and-paste task often determines the speed of the proceedings.

When the dated list is finished the list officer tackles the undated, warned list. These are cases that are moving towards trial but may never actually reach that stage if, say, there is a settlement. Hence it is a difficult list to organise and often leads to argument between clerks and the list officer. The disputes arise from a conflict of viewpoints: the officer's aim is to move as many cases as possible and clear the lists; the clerk's, to prevent cases being taken off the lists. The clerk may be acting on the solicitor's instructions, or it may be that his barrister is engaged on another case, or both.

Before attending a listing session at the QBD a clerk has to prepare thoroughly. He must know his solicitors' needs, the work load of his barristers, and the burdens and needs of other clerks involved in the same actions. The chief list officer usually begins by asking for offers of cases. He may be fortunate and receive one or two offers, but normally most clerks stay silent and wait for him to start selecting cases from the list. On one occasion a clerk did offer a case, much to the surprise of the barrister's clerk on the other side, who objected strongly, claiming that he was not ready to go to trial. The list officer gave him a sympathetic hearing; he knew the objector, but not the other man, who was a Chancery clerk, unfamiliar with QBD procedures. He had mistakenly taken the request for offers at face value, without having consulted his opposite number beforehand. If a case is simple and straightforward it can be offered, but only with the consent of the other side.[6] In another instance a clerk offered such a case, but he had omitted to tell the other side. As it was a relatively straightforward case, all objections were overruled. But the list officer did at least record it as a 'Not before eleven o'clock' listing, allowing the clerk to move his other case, which included the same barrister.

If, as usual, there are no offers, the list officer attempts to 'crack the list' (i.e. clear the queue of cases) by selecting cases himself. He may choose from any part of the list to find cases of suitable length, depending on their complexity and the number of witnesses. The speed at which the list is moving affects the way he treats the excuses and stallings of the clerks. When the courts are busy and cases are being disposed of quickly the clerk of the lists must keep things moving to ensure a steady flow of work to the judges. It is at these times that he is reluctant to stand cases out. Moreover, when a case is rising to the top of the list and is likely to be chosen for hearing, the solicitors to both sides should submit 'consents' to the list officer if they wish to have it stood out. A constant complaint of the QBD clerk of the lists was the lack of advance warning that a consent was to be submitted. One example was a case which the barrister's clerk had successfully been keeping out of the courtroom and in the list. The list officer told him that the court had contacted both parties' solicitors to warn them that trial was imminent but, so far, no consents had been submitted. As a result the case was listed, giving the barrister's clerk and the solicitors about two hours to submit their written consents before the final list was drawn up. On this sort of occasion the list officer knows consents will arrive eventually, so he lists the case as a 'floater' (i.e. due to be heard when the current case in a court is finished). He is trying to impose a deterrent on clerks and solicitors. It rarely works. During one afternoon seven floaters were listed: by the end of the day only two remained after the consents had been sent in. As one clerk put it, the list officer 'just puts the wind up people, which is really silly. He takes a hard line at two o'clock then backs down later on. If he's going to put them in, he should do so.'

Following the QBD listing session, the clerks who have business in the Crown Office go there to organise their Queen's Bench Divisional Court cases. The Divisional Court uses a floating list, so a clerk has little to do other than clarify sone point or ask for a hearing to be expedited. Only a few minutes are spent in the Crown Office.

The next stop is the Court of Appeal (Civil Division). This court has no list officers; the lists are compiled by the clerk to the presiding judge.[7] They are fully floating, that is, no fixtures are made, but some juggling can be done to obtain an approximate indication of when the case might be heard.[8] Judges' clerks are not really part of the same bureaucratic structure as list officers, and each is responsible only to his court of three judges. Contact between clerks and judges' clerks in the Court of Appeal is infrequent. Relations between them may be smooth or rough according to whether the judges' clerk has had experience as a barrister's clerk. The following example shows how matters can go awry. A clerk visited a judge's clerk to discuss the possibility of arranging a hearing date three weeks later. The judge's clerk appeared to ignore the proposal and suggested the following day, as he had a vacancy. The clerk explained that an early date was out of the question, since the transcript of the trial had not arrived, and some forward planning was needed. The judge's clerk agreed to help, but the barrister's clerk did not trust him to arrange proper dates. It was put this way: the judge's clerk was an ex-policeman and he was 'thick', so he was incapable of understanding a clerk's needs. 'He thinks that's the only case we have; he forgets we've got others.' Occasionally a judge's clerk may discuss the planning of a particular appeal directly with his judge.[9]

The final visit of the day is to the office of the Queen's Bench judge in chambers. Here the clerks check the list and make any last-minute arrangements with the judge's clerk. For example, the one who had been given the 'Not before eleven o'clock' listing in the QBD office was able to get the judge's listing changed so that his barrister could appear in both actions. Relations in this office are less formal than in the QBD, and the clerk knew he could rearrange his listing there without much difficulty.

Despite the apparently chaotic manner in which listing is arranged, long-term forward planning is attempted. The most formal process is found in the QBD office. Applications to fix dates for hearings are published in the *Daily Cause List,* notifying the parties of the time at which their application will be heard. Usually clerks attend these hearings with their solicitors or solicitors' clerks (to speak to the issue of the availability of the witnesses). There are lengthy discussions on the probable duration of the trial, the amount of court time available, and some consideration is even given to the likely availability of counsel. The proceedings are conducted quietly, without any joking between the participants, e.g. the list officer is always addressed as 'Mr X.'. In contast, applications to fix dates in the Clerk of the Rules' office and the judge in chambers' office are made in a more lighthearted, informal manner, with everyone joking. Indeed, at times the proceedings appear to be one long joke.

The specialist bars, such as planning or tax, operate a greatly restricted listing procedure in comparison with the general civil law bar. There clerks may only interact with one or two list officers, which allows a greater degree of certainty in arranging business. A clerk of a tax set described the 'settling of the Revenue Paper' (i.e. the High Court revenue trial list): it was arranged once every law term by all the senior clerks of the tax bar—about six in number— with the revenue list officer. It was not a long process, taking only an hour. In addition, this tax clerk dealt with the clerk to the Special Commissioners of the Inland Revenue (a tribunal that hears tax cases). These cases were listed informally and easily: the clerk to the special commissioners was new at his job and dependent on guidance from the tax clerks.

The largest of the specialist civil law bars is the Chancery bar. Clerks who seldom have business in the Chancery Division hold it in some awe because of the complexity imputed to Chancery work. Chancery clerks reinforce this image.[10] Listing is arranged with the Chancery listing officer, and to some extent with the judges' clerks. At one point the Chancery clerks were complaining that the judges' clerks were being obstructive because the Chancery listing officer had been transferred from another division. This internecine struggle would occasionally find expression, for example, when an *ex parte* hearing for an injunction was required urgently; the judges' clerks would delay expedition of the matter.

Besides work in the High Court, Chancery clerks also send their barristers into county courts. County courts, unlike the High Court, are under local control, and this can create problems for the clerk. It means he has to liaise with each court where he has business. The worst aspect for him is the system of fixed hearing dates—fixed without his help. The combined force of the parties can sometimes get a date changed, but clerks generally have little expectation of help from county courts. As one of them put it, the county court officials 'do it just as they please; nothing we say can influence them. Also, it's impossible to try and find out who's responsible for the list. If you phone a court, they just pass you on and on until you *may* end up with someone who knows something about it.' No guidance is given on the time a trial will start; briefs are generally marked 'at 10.30 a.m.', but the case may be second or seventh in the list and may not be heard until late in the day. For the clerk it can mean the waste of a barrister for a whole day. One clerk, for example, had to telephone a county court three times in an effort to find out the position of his case on the list. The most he could extract from the court was that it was 'somewhere near the top'.

LISTING—CRIMINAL LAW[11]

The Courts Act, 1971, converted the Assizes and Quarter Sessions into the present system of Crown courts. Each Crown court has a list officer who, depending on the location of the court, organises his list direct with barristers' clerks, either face-to-face or by telephone. All courts publish a list every afternoon, copies of which are displayed in the List Publication Room at the Law Courts. Some of the centrally located London courts such as the Central Criminal Court, Knightsbridge Crown Court and Inner London Sessions Crown Court distribute their lists to certain key clerks in the Inns of Court so that other clerks can obtain quick notification. By far the most important court for clerks, however, is the Central Criminal Court: it is the only criminal court in London that demands a daily visit from all clerks whose chambers handle criminal work. The remainder need visiting only if dates are to be fixed. One other point should be noted: in the civil courts, clerks generally try to keep cases out of the courtroom; in the criminal courts the main priority is to have the case tried with a minimum of delay.

Clerks who have business at the Central Criminal Court attend the daily listing session at 2 p.m. In comparison with others the office is spacious and well organised. Two of its walls are covered with boards holding cards that carry the names of defendants and the related charges. There are telephones for the clerks' use. The list officers have two small rooms adjoining the main one. When a clerk first enters he greets his colleagues and inspects the cards to acquaint himself with the state of the lists. Most clerks carry a small notebook containing the details of their own cases, which they check against the cards. One or two were quite proud of the systems they had devised to follow the progress of their cases: one clerk, for instance, used numbers, instead of clients' names, to keep track.

Just after 2 p.m. the list officer enters the main room to make up the list for the following day. The procedure is similar to that in the Queen's Bench Division; cases are taken from the warned list and assigned to judges according to the vacancies in the courts and the availability of any 'red' (High Court) judges. Most listing is simple. Clerks can object to cases being put in, although not always with success. The exception occurs when a 'red judge' is allocated to the court; the officer then has to scour the list for suitable cases, such as rape and murder, which are upper-band offences. The effect the sudden appearance of a 'red judge' can have is shown by the case of a clerk who had a rape case listed two weeks earlier than anticipated.

Few suitable cases were available, and no objections were accepted.[12]

Twice a week, sessions are held by the list officer to fix dates for trials. The list is published a week before the fixture session, and if the list is especially full the session is divided into sections of fifteen minutes each. The clerks attending these fixture sessions wait in the main room until the list officer calls out the name of the case. Those involved go into his room and attempt to make the fixture. On occasion the room can be crowded, as it was in one case where there were six defendants, each represented by different counsel. There were six clerks, four senior and two junior, a representative of the Director of Public Prosecutions (DPP), who manages the prosecuting counsel's diary, and a representative of the Metropolitan Police to advise on the availability of police personnel for appearing as witnesses. Planning a fixture is therefore, a complicated business. In one instance where a fixture was being made for March the list officer opened the proceedings by scanning his year chart and announcing, 'I can give you June, July or September.' The clerks looked through their diaries, and a discussion started on the length of the trial. One said his 'governor' had told him it would take three or four weeks, another was adamant that it would last four to six, and finally the DPP's representative claimed that two or three weeks would be enough. After five or ten minutes' discussion a date in September was selected which allowed for a crude median time of three weeks for the trial.

Generally, only senior and first junior clerks attend the Central Criminal Court, but the settling of fixtures at the other London Crown courts is frequently delegated to the second junior. These 'peripheral' courts do not sustain such strong cliques as the Central Criminal Court. The main fom of communication with them is by telephone, as it is also for the Court of Appeal (Criminal Division), where fixing appeals is considered straightforward.[13]

Clerks who do criminal work know that the lists are never entirely stable. A criminal trial can always change: a plea of guilty may turn into a fight (a 'not guilty' plea), witnesses may fall ill or be busy elsewhere. One clerk had his diaries thoroughly worked out when he was told that because of congestion two hundred cases had been moved, from the Central Criminal Court to Reading and Kingston Crown courts. He had no option but to live with the resulting two weeks' chaos until the cases had been relisted.[14] Thus a fixture is always tentative.

LISTING: THE HOUSE OF LORDS AND THE PRIVY COUNCIL

These two courts present exceptionally difficult listing problems. They demand submission to their planning decisions. When the House of Lords sets a date for an appeal it is conditional on the possibility that it may be moved forwards or backwards by a week. This forces the clerk to keep his leader (and possibly a junior barrister) free for at least three weeks. Losing a Queen's Counsel for that length of time has a serious economic impact. There are chambers which do a considerable amount of House of Lords work and are organised with the House's planning requirements in mind. But for most chambers it can be expensive. Not only are fees lost, but tedious explanations have to be made to disappointed solicitors. One clerk asserted that the House of Lords ushers, who are responsible for listing, were impossible to work with. 'When they fix a case, they won't budge.' Another underwent an extreme, though not untypical experience. One of his Queen's Counsel was to argue an appeal on a particular date. The clerk made the necessary arrangements and kept the required period free either side of the date. A short time before the appeal the House of Lords postponed the hearing for twenty days. He objected strongly but the court was inflexible. As a result the barrister's holidays had to be postponed and the clerk had to refuse three murder briefs for him. Again the appeal was moved, and this time the barrister had to delay his honeymoon. An inordinate amount of barristers' time is wasted which, in the clerk's view, is entirely unwarranted. Although clerks have complained, little if anything has been done to remedy the situation.

Occasionally a clerk will have one of his Queen's Counsel appearing in the Lords and the Privy Council. One found himself with a barrister scheduled to appear in both courts on the same day. He appealed to both courts. For a time each claimed superiority, until it was decided that the Privy Council would take precedence and the Lords would rearrange its list.

A clerk is closely involved in the listing arrangements of most courts and can influence the arrangements. With the House of Lords and the Privy Council, however, he is virtually impotent to affect decision-making and must suffer the consequences. The explanation some offered was that the staff of the two courts did not realise the range of clerks' work. None of them had ever clerked, and could not appreciate the difficulties.

ASPECTS OF THE CLERK-LIST OFFICER RELATIONSHIP

As mentioned in the introduction, clerks tend to denigrate list officers (and judges' clerks) as civil servants. Yet the relationship between them can be close. One clerk was best man at a list officer's wedding. Such intimacy is most conspicuous between the criminal law clerks and list officers. On the civil law side a greater distance is kept and the amount of socialising is negligible.

Clerks' central idea of list officers is their unwillingness to work as hard as they do. The civil service structure removes the need to put in a lot of effort. For the clerk the aim of increasing the chambers' business is ever-present. List officers have no comparable goal. One clerk was annoyed to discover the list office of a London Crown court closed for the day at 4.20 p.m.: he was unable to find out where his case would be tried the next day—'the clerks of the lists, all they want to do is the least work possible'. Another if less important belief is in the low intelligence of list officers. A typical view was: 'They're *thick*: no adaptability. They abide by the rules rigidly, but that's not right. The rules are there to be broken and bent. They're in a nine-to-five job and so they think that way.' In pub gossip and elsewhere stories of their stupidity often figure large.

The clerks' antipathy has intensified since the Courts Act of 1971. The Act introduced the bureaucracy which so many of them despise. They liked the direct communication they used to have with the judges' clerks. A senior said:

In the pre-Courts Act days the judges' clerks used to fix the lists. At about 12.30 p.m. the provisional list would come out—the 'flimsy list'. If you had any cases due on at the Assize, you got in touch with the link clerk. At 2.30 p.m. the list for the next day would come out. If you had cases due on at the Assizes at the beginning, you got the 'master plan'. With the civil servants it's all changed . . . *from intelligence to cabbage*. [15]

Clerks' actual behaviour towards list officers seems to contradict their opinion. Besides meeting them in court and talking to them on the telephone, they spend hours with them in the local pubs. It is extremely rare for a list officer to have to buy himself or anyone else a drink when he is in their company. This is one of the most important ways of getting to know list officers. It may lead to preferential treatment. The deference shown them is clear in the following incident. A London Crown court list officer applied for the post of administrator at two other Crown courts. On the day the result would be known—the officer got the job at the less prestigious court of the two—several clerks gathered in a pub to discuss the outcome. One of them said, 'He applied for both, but he really wanted X. court. It's not exactly a proper promotion, more of a *diagonal* promotion.' When word got round that the newly appointed court administrator was on his way to the pub to celebrate, one of the clerks rang some friends to tell them to come and join the party. From the moment the man arrived the clerks bought him round after round of drinks, congratulating him all the while. They did, however, let him buy a bottle of champagne. They promised to visit him at his new court, though it was not in central London and only one of those present had ever been there. In reality probably none of them would, but the intention had to be stated. They remarked that under his authority the court was certain to become less intractable than in the past. When the administrator finally left, they once more fell to discussing his 'mediocre' appointment.

Although judges' clerks are classified as civil servants, they are accorded slightly more respect than list officers, for some of them have been barristers' clerks themselves. Those who have are considered less stupid and are felt to be more responsive to the exigencies of the clerks' duties. Thus when a clerk had to find a High Court judge to hear an *ex parte* appeal for an injunction within the hour he used his network of judges' clerks to find him one.

CONCLUSION

Whenever possible, clerks form close relationships with list officers and judges' clerks. Uppermost in their minds is the possibility that the lists might be scheduled in their favour. For, though the contribution that clerks make to the construction of the lists is substantial, the list officer ultimately controls them. He can speed up or slow down the pace of the list, with powerful effects on the clerks' diaries. He is usually prepared, however, to protect the clerks' 'social territory', that is, to favour those who regularly appear before him as against those who rarely do so.

Thus the development of relations between clerk and list officer depends on proximity. The more distant a court from the clerk's vicinity, and the lower the volume of business he transacts with that court, the less opportunity there is to build up a relationship with the listing personnel. In sum, this aspect of the clerk's work is another element in his aim of making the best and most profitable use of his resources: his counsel.

NOTES

1 Jacob *et al.* (1979), or the 'White Book', as it is popularly known, is a two-volume tome laying down the entire range of procedures used in the Supreme Court. It is the practitioner's 'bible'; every set of chambers possesses a copy or two, which are zealously guarded by the clerks. In 1976 the 'White Book' was priced at £50 without continuation supplements.

2 Beeching (1969: para. 65) commented thus: 'In London, as a result of [. . .] increased demands, the Central Criminal Court is overloaded. We give in Appendix 7 the number of persons, as shown by our special statistical survey, who were committed to the higher courts for trial or sentence and whose cases took longer than 60 days between committal and conclusion. It can be seen that, for criminal trials at the Old Bailey, nearly 70% of all accused persons had to wait longer than the eight weeks recommended by the Streatfield Committee as the period within which a person should be brought to trial, even though 36% of them were in custody. Civil work, too, in London is subject to considerable delay, as can be seen from the fact that there is now a waiting time of eight to nine months for a fixed date in the Queen's Bench Division.' The Royal Commission on Legal Services questioned the Barristers' Clerks' Association at a meeting held on 13 July 1978. One of the witnesses said, *inter alia*, 'We know that at the moment there is a serious backlog of cases awaiting hearing. So it is not just our profession: the whole administration of justice will become extremely expensive if we move away from the present floating system with the disadvantages that it undoubtedly does have, but once you have reported on the matter the public will see the advantages as against the enormous financial cost of doing it any other way, because we have applied our mind as to the other way of dealing with it.'

3 The relevant courts are: House of Lords (including the Judicial Committee of the Privy Council); Court of Appeal (civil and criminal divisions); High Court: Queen's Bench Division, Family Division, Chancery Division, Restrictive Practices Court, Court of Protection, Employment Appeals Tribunal; Crown Court; county courts; magistrates' courts. (Benson 1979: I, table 2.1.)

4   In a personal communication (5 June 1981) the Lord Chancellor's
     Department said, 'Few [listing officers], if any, are ex-barristers'
     clerks.' But no figures were provided.
5   The terminology of listing can be confusing. The main terms used are:
     (a) *fixture,* a case fixed for a particular date subject to the availability of a
     judge; (b) *after fixture* (A.F.), a case recorded as 2 A.F. is the second case
     to be taken after the first fixture for that date is heard. Cases may be
     listed as 1 to 7 A.F.; (c) *K.P.* (keep place), a case which stays out of the
     warned list, by agreement of the parties and the list officer, until the
     date which it is marked 'not before', when it is reinstated in the list at a
     similar point as though it had not been removed; and (d) *floater,* a case
     assigned to a court to be heard after the close of the current case.
6   It should be noted that the Clerk of the Lists has the case files, so that he
     is able to make a superficial judgement on the complexity of the case.
7   Every three weeks a court breaks up and the members form into
     another group of three. Thus virtually every Lord Justice of Appeal has
     an opportunity to be presiding judge, and his clerk is able to arrange the
     lists for his court.
8   In fact a fixture can be made with the consent of all parties, but only
     under special circumstances.
9   For example, in the case of Gouriet *v.* Union of Post Office Workers
     [1977] Q.B. 729, decision reversed in the House of Lords, [1978] A.C.
     435, the appellant, Gouriet, arrived at the Lord Justices of Appeal
     clerks' room at 5.15 p.m. on a Friday afternoon, requesting a hearing
     for the next day, Saturday. The Master of the Rolls, Lord Denning, and
     his clerk decided the case deserved an expedited hearing.
10   In 'Barristers' Diary', *Guardian Gazette,* 25 September 1974: 923, the
     author was moved to write: 'The shadow of Bleak House does not fall
     quite so darkly over the Chancery side as common lawyers still believe
     but some changes should now be made . . . The only people who ever
     seem to be able to find out when and where a summons adjourned to a
     judge, for example, is to be heard are *Chancery barristers' clerks'*
     (emphasis added). See also Oliver and Woolf (1981), *Report of the
     Review Body on the Chancery Division of the High Court.*
11   Clerks with business in both the Law Courts and the Central Criminal
     Court divide the work load between the clerks in chambers, which
     provides for some specialisation in either civil or criminal law.
12   On the problems of delays at the Central Criminal Court see *The Times,*
     7 October 1977; for the difficulties associated with 'red judges' see *The
     Observer,* 9 October 1977.
13   See, however, *The Times,* 21 February 1976, for an article describing
     the occasion when three cases tried by Mr Justice Melford Stevenson
     came up for appeal in the Court of Appeal on the same day, and the
     suspicions that were aroused about the listing process as a consequence.
14   The Barristers' Clerks' Association pressed this point during the
     presentation of its oral evidence to the Royal Commission on Legal
     Services on 13 July 1978: 'It is only occasionally that you know the date
     for the hearing. You have to realise and remember that all the time you

have this running list. A very serious situation that we find these days is that because of the backlog of criminal cases at the moment the Old Bailey are passing cases out to other places, like St Albans. So you could be watching the list at the Old Bailey and suddenly it is transferred to St Albans. It might be a murder case, something quite important, but that is the situation. If you are told it has been transferred to St Albans and the court says it is coming on tomorrow you can say as much as you like, "It is very inconvenient because I have this magistrates' court case for which I had the brief delivered a month ago and my man has read it thoroughly," and they say, "I am very sorry but you must find somebody else to do it." '

15   In the Temple seven clerks whose chambers did considerable business on the seven circuits which the Assizes travelled were designated link clerks. Each clerk liaised closely with the judge's clerk of a particular circuit. The link clerk would receive his Assize list, then other clerks with business on that circuit would request modifications through the link clerk.

Even today a link clerk system exists. Various courts throughout the country send daily lists and warn lists to the link clerks, who then deliver them to the List Publication Room at the Law Courts. At about 4 p.m. the most junior clerk goes to the Law Courts to check the lists for his chambers.

Chapter 6

THE SOCIAL WORLD OF BARRISTERS' CLERKS

In this chapter the relationships formed among barristers' clerks are examined. The emphasis is on their informal relations and networks rather than the more structured groups such as the Barristers' Clerks' Association. The latter is examined in the next chapter. Informal relationships are an extremely important feature of the clerk's world, and I shall be looking at them from several points of view. One point should be borne in mind, however, and that is the very small number of clerks: it generates a degree of interdependence rarely encountered in other occupations.

NETWORKS AND EXCHANGE

A criminal law clerk articulated a central contradiction in clerks' relations when he said, 'Nowhere is there so much competition with so much co-operation. There has to be, otherwise everything would collapse.' In other words, the networks among clerks demand a strict accounting of favours given and owed, and grievances registered and paid off.[1] The co-operative and competitive elements are ever-present in all relationships: one's friends are also one's competitors. The following example is indicative. A fairly senior first junior clerk in a common law set of chambers was checking his case lists for the next day when he noticed that one of the cases had been listed to be heard 'not before twelve noon'.[2] He was surprised and upset, since the fixture had been made without his consent. He telephoned the other clerk in the expectation of receiving an apology. He asked, 'Why didn't you tell the other side what you intended to do? It *is* a matter of courtesy.' The other clerk, a woman, replied that she found such 'formalities' unnecessary. As he put the phone down he remarked, 'Don't worry, I've got their mark, their number.' Then, tapping his head with his finger, 'It's stored up here until the next time.'

The other clerk had offended on several counts. Her most grievous error was in ignoring the convention that fixtures require consultation with all parties. And she should have apologised. Instead she chose to aggravate the situation by her high-handed attitude, even though she was in the wrong. Her failure to make amends reinforced the clerk's attitudes about the unsuitability of women as barristers' clerks and the inferiority of chambers in Lincoln's Inn. Traditionally, Lincoln's Inn houses Chancery lawyers, but there are some common law and criminal law chambers situated there. They are not well liked by clerks in the Temple, being considered second-rate, especially as Lincoln's Inn is a favoured area for the ethnic, or 'ghetto', chambers.[3] Women have always suffered from sexist attitudes among clerks.

Coincidentally, the next call that morning was from a clerk who wanted agreement on a fixture. When the diary had been checked, he was told about the previous caller. They agreed that her behaviour was both deviant and unwarranted. After the second call the clerk commented, 'That's the way it should be done.' Moreover he had granted a favour and was now owed one.[4]

Another point which this incident draws out is the importance of gossip as a means of communication.[5] Barristers' clerks are a small, homogeneous group. They have similar backgrounds and values and spend a considerable amount of time together, either at work or in such settings as listing offices, or informally in pubs. In these settings the main form of communication is talk, and much of it is gossip.

LOCATION AND SPECIALITY

Location and speciality are two variables that affect their network of contacts. Clerks are located, occupationally, in three distinct places: the Temple, Gray's Inn and Lincoln's Inn. To some extent this prevents frequent interaction between clerks from different Inns. They would, for example, use different pubs. Most of their encounters would be at listing sessions or other official occasions.

The second variable has a greater impact on the formation of networks. Clerks whose chambers do the same kind of work have occasion to meet and talk more frequently than those from different specialities. Chancery clerks have little in common with criminal law clerks. The specialist chambers are less numerous and still more restricted. The tax bar, Admiralty bar and planning bar consist of few sets of chambers. But their clerks will have some contact with those from the larger group of civil and commercial law chambers which sometimes send referrals. The divisions between the various groups of chambers were revealed by the questions clerks would ask me. 'What's it like in criminal chambers?' or 'Is it very dull in a tax set?' Some criminal law clerks, for example, were convinced that clerking a tax set required no great effort—an observation which my own experience was unable to support, although the work was of a different nature.

To a limited degree the two variables cut across each other. The Chancery chambers are in Lincoln's Inn, and nearly all the common law chambers are in the Temple and Gray's Inn. Thus interaction between the two broad groups of clerks is doubly restricted.

TYPOLOGY OF RELATIONS

The main analytical distinction I want to draw is between economically based and socially based relationships. The former include what may be termed referral relationships, which exist for the purpose of circulating briefs among chambers; and action sets, which are short-term groupings that arise in order to tackle specific problems (see Boissevain, 1974: 186). Socially based relationships are concerned with the formation and maintenance of cliques and friendships, and are focused mainly on the pubs near the Inns of Court (*ibid.:* 174).

Return circuits. 'Return circuits' are exchange networks created by clerks to cope with the exigencies of barristers' work. A brief may have to be referred to another set of chambers for any number of reasons, and return circuits act as a safety valve for over-pressured clerks. They have other functions, such as assisting unestablished clerks who have not yet generated sufficient work for their chambers.

Hall (1948: 333) wrote that some doctors' referrals 'turn out to be convenient arrangements for sharing fees'. Such arrangements are also to be found among barristers and solicitors, but not among clerks. When a brief is referred to another clerk, so is the clerk's fee. It is the clerk whose barrister actually handles the case who collects the fee. The referrer looks to a return in the future; in passing on a brief he is adding to the stock of favours owed him. Those who share fees receive their reward direct; clerks, however, are rewarded indirectly.

Most clerks believed the return circuits were evidence of the service aspect of their job. They also believed that criticisms by outside observers, such as Bugler (1976) and Zander (1968), of the alleged problems of late returns and overbooking of briefs, were grossly misinformed.[6] Clerks do not regard the referral of briefs as a bad thing: on the contrary, they see it as beneficial to the legal system.

The least contentious type of referral is that between chambers of different specialities. Generally the flow of briefs travels from the generalist to the specialist. The clerk of a tax set received an average of one or two briefs a week from other chambers. He referred all his non-tax briefs to others: 'I phone the other clerk to see if he has someone who can do it, then I get in touch with the solicitor to see if he agrees to that man.' Solicitors sometimes rely on their usual clerks to find them barristers in specialist chambers, especially when they are ignorant of the possible choices. Clerks expect these requests, and deal with them as part of their service. Occasionally a clerk will not know where to place a brief his chambers cannot cope with. At such times he will call a more experienced member of his clique for advice. The trend to more generalist chambers is, however, beginning to reduce the frequency of inter-speciality referrals, except for the most specialised areas such as patent law or Admiralty law.

Switching briefs within a speciality is more problematic than switching between specialities. The ideal is to keep as many briefs as possible in the chambers. Nevertheless, referrals of this nature are necessary when the supply of briefs exceeds the supply of counsel, or when a last-minute crisis in timing prevents a barrister from taking a case up. For example, a plea of guilty might be changed to not guilty, so preventing a barrister from taking on the next case in his diary.

In common law and criminal law chambers such referrals are common, and it is here that the phenomenon of the return circuit is most visible. Small groups of clerks refer briefs between each other almost daily. The key feature of these groups is that the members rely upon and trust each other to provide suitable barristers for the cases. Although they try to be closed circuits, leakages do occur from time to time when the group is unable to deal with all its members' cases. Most of the ones that are referred involve magistrates' court work, simple Crown court work and county court work. High Court business is less frequently referred.

Return circuits come under great stress when last-minute crises occur. The following instances illustrate some of the hazards. A clerk assumed he had safely placed two juvenile court briefs with a colleague. But at five to eleven in the morning he had not been contacted by the barrister intended for one of the cases, which was to begin at twelve noon. He allowed a further five minutes. When the call did not come, he began the search for alternative counsel. By five past eleven he had called three clerks in his return circuit, none of whom could oblige. Although time was short he chose not to contact two sets of chambers outside his return circuit which he knew would have counsel available. Both sets had a particularly poor reputation, for clerks and for barristers. Ten minutes later, at a quarter past eleven, six more attempts had failed. One clerk, hearing of the problem, rang to offer a pupil. The offer had to be refused, since someone with more experience was needed. As the clerk continued calling, another clerk looked in to discuss the Temple football fixtures. He overheard the telephone conversation and said he could provide a barrister immediately. By twenty past the brief had been placed; there was just time for the barrister to reach the court and have a hurried conference with the client. As for the clerk whose barrister had failed to call, he would not necessarily be held at fault but would have been expected to reprimand the barrister.

In the next incident the clerk was virtually powerless to prevent a near disaster. Clerk A.—the senior of a criminal law set—received a call from a barrister, Z., at 11 p.m. It was not one of his own barristers but one to whom he had referred a case. Z. was calling because he was unable, at the last moment, to take the case on, and had not been able to contact his clerk, B., the previous evening. As a result he had telephoned several other clerks to find someone to take his place. He had succeeded, but ought not to have done it himself. If he could not get B. to do it he should have asked A., the referrer. Unfortunately Z. was not conversant with the conventions of the return circuit. To find a replacement he had used his network, which did not correspond with that of the clerks, and A. was disturbed to learn which chambers the brief had gone to. It was one he always avoided unless he was desperate. Nor did he look forward to explaining the new arrangement to the solicitor, since it would reflect badly on himself. Next morning he tried to appease the solicitor, saying, 'Oh, that's fine. He's the *good* one in the chambers, sir.' Nevertheless both of them knew of the chambers' poor repute. And A. was powerless to alter the situation. However, the solicitor, unhappy with the arrangement, found another barrister. He left the task of explaining the removal of the brief to A. 'Terribly sorry, but it was out of my hands.' The situation was successfully resolved for all except the clerk who had lost the brief. A. was glad the solicitor had moved it; he had retrieved his reputation, and he maintained his friendship with the clerk who lost the brief by blaming the solicitor.

Clerks use the return circuits to help the practices of less successful colleagues, usually the younger ones who are just starting. This patronage is fully exploited by all parties, but is often based on friendship.[7] The example of two clerks, Arthur and Bert, shows perfectly the mechanics of such a relationship.[8]

Bert had been in the Temple for thirty years and was senior clerk to a highly regarded common law set of chambers. The chambers had twenty to thirty barristers, with three Queen's Counsel and, at the other end, six pupils in their second six months; in all, a good ladder. Arthur was in his middle twenties and had only been in the Temple a few years. He was senior clerk to a small, weak set of chambers with 'too much tail'. Since Bert's chambers had a good reputation among clerks and solicitors—which Bert attributed to his, not the barristers', skills—the volume of business was large. Each day he would have surplus briefs to refer to other chambers. Most of the referrals were minor cases, mainly remand or bail applications and pleas of mitigation. He was put in the position of having to refer briefs as a result of solicitors not sending in their business until late in the day. They depended on him to find counsel for them, and Bert was proud of the trust in which he was held. He would have from six to nine briefs a day to refer. Arthur's chambers, on the other hand, rarely had enough work to occupy everyone, and he depended on receiving referrals, usually taking the bulk of Bert's returns.

Their relationship developed, however, quite by chance, before Arthur became a senior clerk. When he was a first junior (to a dilapidated set) his senior arranged a conference, involving one of his barristers and a QC from Bert's chambers, which was to be held at Arthur's chambers. This was an elementary breach of etiquette: the conference should have been in the senior counsel's chambers. The result, in Arthur's words, was that 'When it was time for the con.[ference], Bert turned up on the doorstep. He was furious, and Smith [the QC] was behind him, . . . mad, too. Bert gave me a right bollocking, even though it wasn't my fault.'

Despite the fact that he was not to blame, Arthur avoided Bert, to the extent of using pubs little frequented by other clerks. They met again some months later, when Bert began drinking at Arthur's local near the Temple. They chatted, and Bert asked about Arthur's background and the new chambers of which he was senior clerk. He mentioned that he had two extra briefs for a magistrates' court the next day. Had Arthur any spare barristers who could take them? Arthur's barristers handled the cases competently, and Bert, who had been in the same position and knew the problems, began consistently channelling his returns to Arthur. From this inauspicious beginning their friendship and working relationship developed. They met at least once a day, usually at lunchtime, in their local for a drink; and they often met again in the evenings for another.

Despite their friendship, Arthur's supply of returns depended on his providing counsel who could do the work well. That gave him an incentive to vet his intake of barristers carefully and expand the chambers accordingly. On occasion Bert had no spare briefs or Arthur's barristers would be fully occupied. These incidents were taken as part of normal working conditions, and never disturbed the relationship. After some months one or two of Bert's solicitors began to brief Arthur's chambers direct. Arthur was cautious; he made sure that Bert would not be upset and asked his consent first. For he was still dependent on Bert for his supply of work.

Bert also supplied Arthur with barristers as his chambers grew. One ex-pupil had already joined Arthur's chambers, and another was about to do so. A third was taken on as a door tenant only: neither Bert nor Arthur thought his personality suitable, so they gave him a consolation prize. And when Arthur's chambers split into two segments Bert found a set of rooms in the Temple for Arthur's segment. Arthur commented, 'Bert knows people who know people in the right places.'

Arthur's dependence was never openly discussed, though both were plainly aware of it. But they sometimes joked about their relationship. When arrangements were being made for Bert's group, which included Arthur and his wife, to attend a BCA dinner and dance, someone asked about the price of the tickets. As Arthur was Bert's guest, Arthur said, 'Don't insult Bert. I depend on him for my bread and butter.' An analogy can be drawn here with the position of a Scottish senior advocate, who is expected to pay the bus fares of his junior colleagues (Wilson, 1965).

Bert was almost paternal towards Arthur. In one respect his attitude was odd. Many clerks considered Arthur an outsider, since he had not entered clerking until he was in his early twenties. As a result he did not spend much time in their company. Gradually, under Bert's patronage, he came to be accepted, and his attitude changed too. Bert also benefited from the relationship. He had gained a friend, he had a reliable home for his returns, and he had somewhere to send his ex-pupils. In other words, his solicitors were satisfied and he maintained esteem among young barristers. One key point about this type of relationship is that it endures. It takes time to develop and mature.

Action sets. In contrast to referral networks, occasional short-term relationships are established to solve particular problems. The members of these action sets may be drawn from within or outside a clique (Boissevain, 1974: 186). One of the earliest action sets on record came together in 1882. A clerk brought an action in the Westminster County Court against his late employer for half a crown. The report mentions that '. . . the case created considerable interest among barristers' clerks, and it appeared that the action had been brought at the request of a number of clerks in the Temple'.[9] Several clerks appeared as witnesses for the plaintiff, including a clerk to a Court of Appeal judge. More recent examples include the formation of the Barristers' Clerks' Association in 1922 to simplify the problem of buying wreaths for deceased clerks. The BCA soon developed a wider range of activities and exchanged its action-set structure for a more permanent form. On one occasion the Chancery clerks came together to draw up a blacklist of solicitors who had defaulted on fees. The intention was to boycott them, but it failed. The group was too large and lacked sufficient cohesion.

The commonest reason for the formation of action sets is to settle fee-levels where several barristers from different chambers are involved in the same case. One civil law clerk, who had a junior barrister appearing in a heavy case involving several Queen's Counsel, waited for the clerk of his barrister's leader to fix his fee before submitting his own. The leader's clerk negotiated £3,250 on the brief and £250 a day refreshers:[10] the junior's clerk charged a £2,000 brief fee and £150 a day refreshers. He pointed out, 'In a sense I'm following the old two-thirds rule.'[11]

The most difficult struggles are with the taxing officers of the Crown courts when settling the fees for legally aided criminal cases (see Graham-Green, 1973). In one case which involved four Queen's Counsel, two of the clerks were indignant at the low fees granted on taxation. After several telephone calls and visits to the court they had failed to extract any increase. They believed the taxing officer was waging a personal war on fee levels in general, and they were in the front line. They joined forces for the appeal against the taxation. In their letters of appeal, drafted separately but compared and then redrafted, they wrote:

> The learned judge thought that the case was a grave one; he showed this by granting four certificates for leading briefs and reflected that view in the very severe sentences imposed. A criticism has been made that there should not have been four leading counsel in the case. It would appear that this view has been taken into account in assessing the fees.
>
> Mr Smith [QC] tells me that this is the first time in his recollection that he has ever been required to make an all-out attack on a number of police officers on the lines that the written and signed confessions were obtained by beatings and threats. He found this an extremely heavy burden with many officers and the task of presenting a balanced approach to so delicate a problem required a sustained detailed consideration of every question asked of each witness. Mr Smith found the case rather exhausting and required his working every day both before and after court and even during the lunch, morning and afternoon breaks.
>
> The fees are in my experience (thirty years) the lowest I have ever seen for a leader for a case of this kind. The sheer amount of work put into it by both the leaders and juniors, and which it demanded, called for a substantially higher brief fee and refreshers than allowed.

The second clerk wrote:

> It was very kind of you to meet us. I know both Mr Smith's clerk and myself were very surprised at the amount allowed, this being £400 on the brief and £100 a day.
>
> On my own behalf I would like to say that Mr Brown's [QC] working day on this case started at 6.30 a.m. and finished at 6.15 p.m. when he arrived back at chambers and I do feel that this has not been properly taken into account.
>
> Mr Brown tells me that the defence did their best to shorten the case by consenting to the trial going ahead on one count only so that all other counts

were left on the File. I understand that the trial could well have been double the final length.

I do feel that it should be borne in mind that even in the 1930s and '40s Queen's Counsel were being paid brief fees 100 guineas or more and that ten times that figure in 1976 would be comparable. Which would mean that the brief fee we should be talking about should be £1,000 or more. A guideline might be rent and rates in the Temple in those times were approximately £500 and are certainly over £5,000 now.

When Mr Smith's clerk and I went to . . . and you were kind enough to see us, I referred to a brief fee of £850 on the brief and refreshers of £150 a day (which included 'the long days') referred to as being the minimum that Mr Brown would consider on a private brief. Indeed he would have expected a private agreed brief fee of £2,500 and £250 a day, which would fit in with my calculation above.

After threatening to take the matter further the two clerks succeeded in persuading the tax office to double the original fees. Their concerted action had been successful. Action sets, then, are an everyday feature of a barrister's clerk's life, and they demonstrate the high level of interdependence that obtains.

Social relations. It is difficult to separate the social from the economic in barristers' clerks' lives. They hardly ever relax from their work, even when they are ostensibly socialising. But their most significant social activity is drinking. Indeed, alcohol plays an important role in the entire legal profession. The pub or wine bar creates an atmosphere that promotes talk and gossip, and is an essential forum for clerks and lawyers. In the Temple, for example, the entrances carrying the heaviest pedestrian traffic are bounded by pubs. Among clerks each pub has its own group of devotees. The choice of pub is partly dictated by proximity. The west claims those from Paper Buildings and King's Bench Walk; the east claims those from the area round Middle Temple Lane. One of the main determinants in the choice of pub, however, is the purpose a clerk has in mind. Two pubs are primarily clerks' pubs, where lawyers are seldom seen, and it is in these that the serious Friday-night drinking sessions take place. There are pubs which are used mainly by lawyers and journalists. Between the two extremes there is one which is used by both clerks and lawyers, but the two groups keep apart, and it attracts younger rather than older clerks. One pub, however, stands apart. In general it is barristers' territory but there is a central hallway where clerks will stand drinking and watching everyone who comes and goes. If a clerk is with a barrister they use a bar rather than the corridor.[12]

Within these broad limits different cliques of barristers' clerks have allegiances to various pubs. One group, having used the same establishment for years, were allowed to serve themselves from behind the bar, and every Friday night the landlady cooked them a meal. Barristers were excluded from the group, but if one did join, the conversation became formal and stilted until he had left. There were rare exceptions. A clerk brought one of his barristers, who practised in the North, to a Friday-night session. The barrister had recently converted from being a solicitor, when he used to brief the clerk's chambers. As he was in London to eat his dinners, his occasional presence did not pose a great threat to the sanctity of the clique.[13] The only other outsiders admitted were solicitors' clerks, who supply work and are of equivalent status to barristers' clerks.

The atmosphere of a pub is most important. When the landlord of one pub died, the clerks who used it all felt that the atmosphere deteriorated. Collective inertia deterred them from leaving, even though they complained about the new management, until one of them was banned for arguing with the head barman and the new landlady.[14] 'We left a lot of beer on the deck that night.' The group gradually re-formed on the other side of the Temple. The new venue was an improvement on the old because it provided greater privacy. The doors were locked at 9 p.m., and those who stayed on could continue drinking until the early hours. Since Friday night was devoted to drinking, everyone's behaviour became freer. Once, after hours, they played a game of rugby, two of them going home with a limp and one having to wear dark glasses for several days to hide a black eye.

The role of the pub to those engaged in the law is best defined by analogy: it is what the coffee house was to the eighteenth century, a centre for the exchange of information. Another is the courts, especially the Royal Courts of Justice and the Old Bailey.

Civil and Chancery clerks meet most mornings in the coffee rooms of the Royal Courts of Justice. There are usually some solicitors' clerks present who either sit and talk with the barristers' clerks or form their own group on the other side of the room. The general pattern is for clerks to drift in and out: those who arrive first buy their coffee and leave the change with the cashier as part payment towards the next clerk's refreshment, and so on. The conversation focuses on business—fees, governors—although occasionally they meet to discuss more specific problems. The coffee room is particularly suitable, since it is one of the few places where clerks from all fields of law congregate, and assistance can be sought beyond the normal confines. For example, a young common law clerk waited until he was alone with an older, more experienced Chancery man so that he could air the difficulties he was having with a barrister he believed was about to have a nervous breakdown. But on the everyday, commonplace level, because these coffee-room meetings are independent of the normal cliques, the talk is constrained and more inhibited than in a pub: it deals with the general and only rarely with specifics.

Old Bailey meetings are different again. They are a by-product of work at the Old Bailey. Those who meet in the Law Courts do so for their own sake. The courts are close to the Inns, and provide a convenient centre. The Old Bailey is too distant to be a casual meeting place. The snack bar is heavily used by those connected with the court, such as lawyers, police, witnesses and the public. There is little privacy, whereas meetings at the Law Courts are timed for periods when the coffee room is least used.

Barristers' clerks come together in other places as well. One group of five or six took a day trip abroad each year. They would set out on a boat train early in the morning, start drinking on the Channel ferry, then walk, talk, eat and drink throughout the day, returning late at night, often missing the last train from Dover and instead hiring a taxi to London. On a larger scale the Barristers' Clerks' Association organises an annual dinner-dance at a London hotel, which is generally well attended.

The role of Masonic lodges is important in establishing contacts between clerks. However, I was never able to ascertain direct the extent of the importance. Only hints and occasional comments gave any indication.

The other main social activity is sport. Each year the clerks play the Bar at cricket at the Oval. They arrange golf and tennis matches, but the most popular sport is football. A team drawn from the Temple competes in the London Legal League, and plays an annual match against the Lincoln's Inn clerks. Bowker noted that these inter-Inn matches have been a regular event since 1909, when the Temple won four–nil, 'and if my memory serves me, I think I am right in saying that our friends of the Chancery Side have never won a single match of this series' (1947: 23).[15] In addition, five-a-side matches are played between teams from various buildings within the Temple.

CONCLUSION

One clerk spoke of his involvement in all these activities as benefiting him thus: 'When they've got some surplus work, I'll hope they'll think of me and pass it over.' Despite the social gloss, relations between clerks are in fact a means of establishing and maintaining business. Moreover, although barristers' clerks see themselves as independent, self-sufficient individuals, few are. They are bound together by reciprocal obligations.

These different relationships also exert pressure to conform.[16] No outsider can hope to stay in the business for long unless his field of law is so specialised that he can remain independent of the others, or his work does not rely on the same sources.[17] Conformity is important.

NOTES

1 Cf. Boissevain (1974: 25).
2 See chapter 5.
3 See chapter 3 and Benson (1979: I, para. 35.3).
4 Cf. Goffman (1956), Mills (1940) and Homans (1958).
5 Paine proposed that 'a working definition of gossip would include: 1. talk of personalities *and* their involvement in events of the community, and 2. talk that draws out other persons to talk this way. For a gossiper usually endeavours to receive more than he gives. He has "long ears" and part of his art lies in arranging a constant flow of information to himself. This argument does not deny that a gossiper, still with the intention of receiving more than he gives, often distributes information.' (Emphasis in original.) (1967: 283). But see Gluckman (1968) and Handelman (1973); for a discussion within a legal context, see Lewis (1976).
6 See the oral evidence of the Barristers' Clerks' Association to the Royal Commission on Legal Services, 13 July 1978.
7 Boissevain (1966: 18) defines patronage as 'the complex of relations between those who use their influence, social position or some other attribute to assist and protect others, and those whom they so help and protect' (footnote omitted). Blok (1969: 365) prefers a transactional emphasis in in his definition: 'Patronage, then, is a structural principle which underlies asymmetric, personal transactions involving protection and loyalty between two persons or groups of persons. By

definition, transactions refer to those sequences of interaction which are governed by reciprocity' (footnote omitted).

8   These are pseudonyms.

9   Lyster *v*. Spearman (1882) 12 L.T. Jo. 391.

10   The brief fee covers the preparation, and the conduct of the case for the first day. Refreshers are payments for subsequent appearances in court. See Boulton (1975: 50) and the Senate (1980: para. 120).

11   See Abel-Smith and Stevens (1967: 223–5) and Benson (1979: I, para. 33.75). The rule was abrogated by the Bar in 1971.

12   These descriptions are simplified to point out the salient features. The pubs are not so exclusive in reality.

13   To qualify for call a student barrister must keep terms, of which there are four in a year, by dining at his or her Inn on at least thirty-six occasions. See Benson (1979: I, para. 38.43).

14   The clerk and two others gatecrashed a private party being held in a room over the bar. The landlady ejected them, and while they were waiting for a taxi the argument broke out between the clerk, who was from the Irish Republic, and the barman, who was from Northern Ireland. This accentuated their disagreement. The ban lasted for roughly two months. See appendix 1.

15   During the second world war the Temple *v*. Lincoln's Inn match fell into abeyance and was not revived until 1962.

16   See Shibutani (1955, 1962), Turner (1954) and Urry (1973).

17   For example, see the evidence of the Wellington Street chambers submitted to the Royal Commission on Legal Services.

Chapter 7

THE BARRISTERS' CLERKS' ASSOCIATION

In outlining the history and role of the Barristers' Clerks' Association I have relied upon the BCA's annual reports 1949–76 and published and unpublished papers, as well as interviews with past and present officers and members. Unfortunately it was not possible to obtain access to the minute books of the management committee's meetings.[1] This description must, therefore, be less than thorough.

THE BEGINNING

The association was founded in 1922 for the purpose of rationalising the collection of funds for wreaths for dead clerks and gifts for those about to retire. These 'whip-rounds' for funds were usually carried out by a few active clerks, but the process was considered inefficient because the amounts in question did not justify the energy expended. The clerks also felt that the casual form of the collection was unsuited to the nature of the occasion, and so, as a past chairman put it, they 'dignified the procedure'. After its formation the association broadened its ambit to include matters of etiquette and discipline. The members never considered it a trade union; earnings were assumed to be the concern of clerk and principal alone.

Meetings were held in a room in the Royal Courts of Justice: its use had been granted by the Lord Chancellor's Office in 1920, originally as a common room for clerks whose names were entered on 'the Register' (Annual Statement of the Bar, 1920: 6). The years between 1922 and 1949 are virtually devoid of written records, and most of the officers of those early years are retired or dead.[2] During that period the BCA moulded itself into its present basic structure of a management committee of senior clerks drawn from common law, Chancery and provincial chambers, with a smaller sub-committee of junior clerks, and a committee for the benevolent fund. In 1954 the annual report carried the retirement notice of Ernest Young, which outlines the type of character the BCA depended on its early years:

. . . one of the most outstanding of our colleagues and one to whom we all owe a great debt. A man of great character, his dignified bearing and the complete trust he enjoyed of Bench and Bar has done a tremendous amount to enhance the status of Barristers' Clerks. He was a founder, prime mover and adviser of this Association. It was to him that individual clerks took their troubles, knowing that their confidences were secure and that the valuable guidance they received would be sound and wise. [AR, 1954: 13]

The present series of annual reports began in 1949. The statement of accounts for that year shows that only two guineas were spent on wreaths: the largest sum, £25, went to the clerks' sports club, while printing costs absorbed the next largest amount, £18. In the twenty-seven years since its inception the association had redirected its concern from the dead to the living.

The annual report of 1949 is especially forthcoming about the values and principles of the BCA. The stimulus for this exegesis came from the Evershed Committee on Supreme Court Practice and Procedure. The association felt it necessary to defend itself against attack; in fact the management committee was frightened, as the opening sentence of the annual report shows: 'The Chairman's Report last year drew attention to rumours of revolutionary changes which might affect our members . . .' (AR, 1949: 2). In accordance with its defensive stance, the BCA submitted two memoranda to the Evershed Committee which attempted to justify the role and position of the barrister's clerk. The memoranda and annual report provide interesting contrasts; the former is designed to teach the committee about clerks, while the latter was intended to be read by clerks. But the report, too, had didactic elements. The main part was devoted to the topic of the clerk's fee.

It is the clerk's function to relieve the barrister of [administration]. Counsel has always been paid an honorarium and it became customary for the clerk also to receive an honorarium to see that the services to be rendered by Counsel were in fact carried out. Clerks are of assistance both to the lay client and to Solicitors. [AR, 1949: 2–3]

The consequences of the abolition of the clerk's fee would be:

The abolition of any relationship between the remuneration of barrister and his clerk would virtually result in the abolition of the clerk, the interests of

the clerk and the interests of his chambers being so interwoven that the
system of representation by counsel, as it is known today, would break
down, and the consequences of these changes would be very harmful to the
public at large. [AR, 1949: 4]

Throughout, the BCA was emphasising the uniqueness of
barristers' clerks. For example, against attacks from the Solicitors'
Managing Clerks' Association, which said in its memorandum to
the Evershed Committee that 'clerks' fees should be abolished', the
BCA replied:

The fact that solicitors' clerks work hard and well on a salary basis [should]
not be taken as a criterion [for the abolition of clerks' fees]. The whole
position is different. A solicitor's clerk has security in his office and often a
pension scheme. If one of the partners in his firm dies suddenly, the clerk's
position will be unaffected, as the firm would carry on; but if counsel dies
suddenly, or is promoted to the Bench, then the clerk may be left without a
principal. [AR, 1949: 5–6]

The BCA's representative tried to persuade the committee that
clerks were level-headed, sensible men who would never be
influenced by mere financial considerations.[3] It further argued that
clerks were on equal terms with barristers: 'The relationship [of clerk
and counsel] is far removed from the ordinary one of Master and
Servant and approximates to that of a partnership.'

But the anticipated support of the Bar was missing. Mr Casswell,
KC, the representative of the Bar Council, in his oral evidence to the
Evershed Committee, said the BCA memorandum had distorted the
level of barristers' fees upwards by choosing successful barristers
instead of a representative sample. The Bar Council also said that the
clerk's fee was an anachronism.

The veil was lifted with the publication of the Evershed report
(1953). In sum, the report recommended the abolition of the clerk's
fee, expressing the hope that this would not lead to an increase in
fees; and that there ought to be more discussion between solicitor
and barrister on fees, but that the actual fixing of junior counsel's fees
should remain in the hands of the clerk. The BCA received the
recommendations stoically:

In the annals of the Association the past year can be said to have produced
few surprises. True, the Final Report of the Committee on Supreme Court
Practice and Procedure . . . has been published with recommendation
which if acted upon might have important repercussions on Barristers'
Clerks, but until those recommendations which affect us most' are

implemented, (if at all), we do not think any useful purpose would be served by a lengthy discussion on the subject in this Report. Sufficient to say, that your Committee are co-operating with the General Council of the Bar, who have kindly met your representatives, and whatever the outcome, we shall together, we feel sure, arrive at a solution which will do justice to the Bar on the one hand and our members on the other. [AR, 1953: 2]

The clerk's stoicism was rewarded, for, as Zander (1968: 88) wrote, 'the majority of [Evershed's] numerous recommendations have been ignored.'

CONTROL AND DISCIPLINE

During its dealings with the Evershed Committee the BCA saw an opportunity to advance its control over clerks:

. . . it became increasingly obvious that the Working Party [of the Evershed Committee] were anxious to obviate any possibility of individual clerks falling below the high standard of integrity which is the proud boast of our members, and a statement by your Chairman that it was hoped to place our Association on a high level with disciplinary powers over its members, was enthusiastically received by Sir Raymond Evershed and his Working Party. [AR, 1949: 6]

The means to this end was to convert the BCA into an Institute of Clerks to Barristers, 'with the object, among others, of raising the status of a barrister's clerk to something commensurate with the importance of this highly specialised, important and responsible profession' (AR, 1949: 10), and increasing the BCA's powers to include disciplinary matters. One benefit of the change would be the eradication of the Dickensian image of black-coated clerks sitting at high desks with quill pens. Nothing resulted from the proposal.

Nevertheless the BCA continued trying to extend its authority over clerks, even though it had no effective powers. Thus in the case of a clerk who left one set of chambers for another and wrote to his former chambers' solicitors, asking them to transfer their business, the only sanction it could impose was a severe reprimand. The clerk did not even appear for his reprimand (AR, 1951: 4–5).

In addition to disciplinary powers the BCA wanted, in effect, a closed shop: senior clerks should be selected from experienced clerks only. The report for 1956 notes:

As the result of information which the Committee had received as to the appointment of an inexperienced person as a Barristers' Clerk to northern

Chambers, it was thought necessary to communicate with the Bar Council to prevent such a happening in the future. [AR, 1956: 5]

There were other instances: two secretaries and a solicitor's clerk had been appointed senior clerks. The junior clerks' section of the BCA management committee objected strongly to the usurpation of their natural rights. The solicitor's clerk who became a barrister's clerk especially angered them. On his first day as a senior he was overheard in the coffee room of the Law Courts saying that the job was 'a piece of old rope, there was nothing to it'. The junior clerks persuaded the BCA management committee to take action, and a sub-committee was set up to study the problems of outsiders becoming senior clerks. But the juniors found it difficult to convince the sub-committee that the problem was real. Eventually the BCA recommended to the Bar Council that all senior clerks should be clerks of at least three years' standing and members of the BCA. The Bar Council rejected the notion because the BCA was unable to guarantee a constant supply of clerks, especially in the provinces. But the Council agreed, in principle, that senior clerks ought to be experienced.[4]

PENSIONS AND JUDGES' CLERKS

For several years, 1951 to 1965, two issues predominated in the annual reports: pensions and the position of barristers' clerks *vis-à-vis* judges' clerkships. The fluid and fragmented character of chambers had always militated against a secure pension arrangement. The Bar claimed that chambers were not cohesive units similar to corporations, and, as a result, no structure existed that could assume responsibility for pensions. The burden was the clerk's alone. In 1951 a scheme was introduced to improve the situation. The pension scheme was managed by a pension service company and could be funded by clerks only, or principals only, or by the two jointly. It was attractive in that both principal and clerk could obtain tax relief on the contributions. Although the scheme is promoted by the BCA, it has never been very successful. And at the annual general meeting in 1977 the members voted not to opt out of the State pension scheme.[5]

Judges' clerks were generally barristers' clerks appointed to that position by a principal on his elevation to the Bench. It is a form of semi-retirement. A judge's clerk's day is short and his duties are moderate in their demands, since his attention is concentrated on one person. He fills the role of intermediary between judges and the rest of the legal profession. But his position was not officially sanctioned. When a judge died or retired, his clerk had also to retire, without a secure pension. From 1951 to 1954 discussions were held between the Bar, judges, judges' clerks, barristers' clerks and the government which resulted in the passing of the Supreme Court Officers (Pensions) Act, 1954. The Act established the position and pensions of judges' clerks, among others. The BCA applauded it as 'undoubtedly the outstanding event of 1954' (AR, 1954: 2). In the years following the BCA attempted to secure the Lord Chancellor's agreement that future judges' clerks would be selected from the ranks of barristers' clerks. It wanted a closed shop for a secure, pensionable post.

The clerks had not found the government sympathetic during the debates on the pension Bill. The Attorney General, Sir Lionel Heald, in his opening speech on the second reading, said, '. . . if [judges'] clerks were to be made pensionable it was not possible any longer for the judge on his appointment to retain the right to nominate his own clerk and take him with him.'[6] He reinforced the argument by pointing out, 'The judges took the view that, in order to get the pensions for their clerks, which they were anxious to do, they were bound to give up their right of patronage or nomination.'[7]

But in preparation for this debate the BCA lobbied fifty barrister MPs. MPs who participated in the debate rallied to the clerks' cause, specially in the matter of retaining the judges' patronage. And so the encomiums flowed.

I think that everybody who had practised in the profession will feel a deep debt of gratitude to the barristers' clerks and the judges' clerks for the smoothness with which their professional engagements can be carried out. A great deal depends on the knowledge of, and the mutual co-operation between, judges' clerks on the one side, with their knowledge of the practical workings of the profession, and barristers' clerks on the other.[8]

Mr Scholefield Allen deplored the severance of the relationship between clerk and principal, which he described as

. . . perhaps one of the most intimate relationships which exists either in the professions or the world of commerce. I doubt whether there is a more intimate relationship than that which exists between the barrister and his clerk, and suddenly to sever it when the master goes to the bench is deplorable.[9]

He knew, however, where to lay the blame. He upbraided the Treasury for being 'the nigger in the woodpile'.[10] But the Attorney General gave an assurance that the Lord Chancellor intended to appoint from the ranks of barristers' clerks.

At first the BCA was buoyant, even though it had failed to secure the judges' patronage. But a year later it reported despondently:

The regulations made under the Act implement this assurance by referring to the *desirability* of applicants having had at least five years' experience as a Barrister's Clerk, and in view of the many statements made in the House during the passage of the Bill in question on both its second and third readings . . . we entertained at that time no doubt that Barristers' Clerks would in fact invariably be appointed to any vacancy which might occur among Judges' Clerks. Such, however, has not proved to be the case, for of the six appointments which have been made, two of these have been of applicants who have had no experience as Barristers' Clerks. [AR, 1955: 3]

The significance of these two appointments was that it was the *judges* who chose the 'outsiders', not the Lord Chancellor's Office or the Treasury. The recruiting procedure was such that after a short list had been drawn up and preliminary interviews held, the final decision was made by the judges alone. The clerks' fears had been of the administrative obstacles that might be put in their way, not of the judges' choice. After senior officers of the BCA had met the Lord Chancellor, the Lord Chief Justice and the Attorney General, they felt able to report that, given suitable candidates, all future judges' clerks would be expected to have had experience as barristers' clerks. And the BCA would receive advance notice of the vacancies before they appeared in the press.

In the following year, 1956, two judges' clerks were appointed, and to the relief of the BCA both were barristers' clerks. However, between 1957 and 1965, when the last mention of judges' clerks occurs in the annual reports, the controversy continued. In 1957 the Lord Chancellor's Office neglected to bring up to date its list of potential applicants, so that a non-clerk was appointed. Again the BCA had interviews with the Lord Chancellor. The same year the judges' clerks formed their own association: it naturally forged strong links with the BCA and co-operated with it to ease the way for barristers' clerks to transfer from one side to the other.[11]

By 1965 the familiar complaints were again being heard, but this time, it seemed, too few barristers' clerks had applied. One explanation for the decline in applicants was the growth of legal business and the expansion of the Bar during the 1960s. It was no longer worthwhile giving up a lucrative career for the relatively low salary of a judge's clerk.[12] As the statistics show, judges' clerks have remained a heterogeneous group.[13]

RESISTING ATTACKS

Until the late 1950s barristers' clerks were not a conspicuous occupational group. But from 1959 onwards they have been a regular object of criticism. The first was about business efficiency.

Towards the end of [1959] the legal profession, not least of all the Bar and their Clerks, were astonished by the contents of an Editorial in *The Times* newspaper severely criticising the business efficiency of many barristers' Chambers. [AR, 1959: 5]

The *Times* leader had said, 'The office inefficency of many barristers' chambers is a disgrace to a profession. This is because they are run not by barristers, but by their clerks, who are wholly untrained in business methods.'[14] The article recommended the use of business efficiency experts to improve the situation.

In a reply the chairman of the BCA did not dispute the facts:

We do not shrink from criticism but to assert that barristers' chambers are inefficiently managed by the clerk is wholly unjustified.

We defy any business efficiency consultant to learn the multifarious duties of a barrister's clerk without many years of training and experience.

The peculiar personal relationship which exists, and has existed for generations, between the barrister and his clerk is something that both the Bar and the clerks cherish.

In spite of what ill-informed persons write in the Press, we are proud in playing a small part in the administration of justice in this country which is acknowledged to be the best in the world.[15]

Needless to say, the General Council of the Bar and the Treasurers of the Inns of Court rallied to the clerks' side in the letters page, on the principle that dog does not eat dog in public. The BCA came unharmed out of this skirmish with the press.

The next round of criticism was a year later. In a television documentary, 'The lawyers', 'a solicitor made some caustic and unwarranted remarks' (AR, 1960: 12). Some members of the management committee wanted to ignore them. But the audience had comprised seven million people, the committee asked the producer to alter the film on future showings. He refused, pointing out that it also reported favourable comments.

The clerks' sensitivity to criticism grew. In 1964 the Law Society sent a confidential memorandum to the Bar Council which contained criticisms of the Bar and included barristers' clerks and their fees.[16] After extensive discussion, the Bar Council and the Law Society published a joint statement which said, among other things, that the abolition of clerks' fees would not be in the public interest. But the BCA made certain that its own views had been articulated in a counter-memorandum.

Michael Zander attacked the restrictive practices of the legal profession in 1968. He criticised barristers' clerks as untrained, over-powerful and too highly paid at the expense of the client. On this occasion the chairman of the Bar Council, Desmond Ackner, rebutted the criticisms. 'The statement that the clerk controls the flow of work in chambers and its distribution to the different barristers working there is, for the most part, false.'[17]

Since that time there have been occasional articles in the press (e.g. Bugler, 1976) reiterating the essence of Zander's criticisms. They culminated in the announcement of a Royal Commission on Legal Services in 1976.[18] The BCA submitted a detailed memorandum of evidence, setting out the tasks performed by barristers' clerks and defending them against the main criticisms.

THE RISE OF PROFESSIONALISM

In the 1960s the BCA intensified its drive for professional status. Everett Hughes (1958: 45) has argued that members of an occupation have ideal models of what constitutes a profession. For the BCA the model was the Bar. There were three areas which it was interested in improving: control and discipline of members, raising educational standards, and improving business efficiency.

Control and discipline over its members have always eluded the BCA. The main reason is structural. It is the barrister who is responsible for the actions of his or her clerk.[19] The sanctions open to the BCA are reprimands, demotion from qualified (full) to associate membership, and expulsion. The annual reports provide no statistics on the number of cases handled by the disciplinary sub-committee. The secretary of the BCA told me of three cases. In the first, a clerk circulated letters to solicitors outlining the specialities of his barristers. He was suspended from the BCA for a few months for touting, then reinstated. The second involved a clerk who, after accepting a defence brief, discovered that his barrister had agreed to prosecute in the same case. He returned it, and the defendant's solicitors complained about the barrister they had chosen appearing for the prosecution. Boulton (1975: 24–5) expressly states that the barrister (or clerk) should discuss a conflict of this nature with the defendant's solicitor, and the clerk in this case had not done so. He was suspended and made to attend the lectures for associate members, then reinstated. In the final case a solicitor complained about the late return of a brief. But the clerk retired before the matter was taken up by the disciplinary committee.

Control is also enforced informally. Bugler (1976: 287) cites the example of a salaried barrister's clerk who was persuaded to adopt a percentage commission instead of a salary. The secretary of the BCA said, however, that she had not been coerced into it. A member of the management committee had simply explained that the clerk was entitled, as of right, to a five per cent commission.

The move towards raising educational standards came out of 'the desirability to strengthen our Association and lay down qualifications for membership' (AR, 1967: 3).[20] But Benson (1979: I, para. 34.39) felt that more training could be given in accounting and office management, and that barristers should ensure adequate standards of training and experience for their clerks.

The desire to improve business efficiency resulted from a suggestion to the Bar Council by the Lord Chancellor that the BCA 'might consider what form of bookkeeping is best for Counsel's Chambers' (AR, 1966: 7). Instead of employing outside consultants, to whom there had been objections in 1959, the BCA decided to undertake the task itself. The motivating force was Sydney Newland, the chairman, who had been in local government since the second world war. His local council had set up its own Organisation and Methods team, and he believed a similar approach could be taken to the organisation of clerks' work in chambers.

> One of the most important matters which the association is at the moment undertaking is an Organisation and Methods Survey.
> Counsel's Chambers are usually depicted in films, and on television, exactly as they might have been in Dickensian times, with perhaps the addition of one telephone and one typewriter. The methods employed by the Clerks are thought to be just as antiquated. Nothing could be further from the truth . . . [AR, 1967: 6]

The twenty people involved in the project formed study groups to

look at the finance and bookkeeping of chambers, the searching of
court lists, telephone systems and the control of staff. The team
reported in 1969, and a year later its findings were published as a
Mehods Manual for Counsel's Clerks (BCA, 1970), 'a . . . guide to
assist [young clerks] in training to become qualified barristers'
clerks' (p.v). The BCA had high hopes of its manual:

. . . there is no doubt that it supplies what is considered to be a long felt
want. Now for the first time the junior clerk who aspires to higher office can
ascertain by a knowledge of the Manual, something of the subjects in which
he has to become proficient. No longer will he be dependent on the good
offices of his senior clerk to instruct him, neither will he need to learn, as did
many of his predecessors before him, by trial and error. [AR, 1970: 2]

In combination with Boulton (1975) it became the basic text for the
training of junior clerks. But it never did or could replace the tutelage
of the senior clerk. Moreover within a year the Courts Act, 1971,
had rendered a third of the manual obsolete, and no revisions were
made. Thus it fell quietly into disuse. Even some members of the
management committee thought it had been a waste of time and
effort.[21] The manual was to have been revised in 1976, but the
advent of the Royal Commission on Legal Services forestalled any
action. With the introduction of computers into chambers a new
edition would probably again become obsolete.[22]

In its quest for autonomy and self-regulation, and raising
educational standards, the BCA has had only qualified success.
Educational standards are improving, and more junior clerks are
enrolling for the lecture courses. But it has not been able to introduce
minimum entry qualifications, and entry still depends largely on
informal networks. Nor has the BCA had any success in exercising
disciplinary control. Membership is not obligatory, and loss of
membership has a negligible effect on a clerk's career. And the
association has never surmounted the obstacle that the barrister is the
clerk's final authority, not the BCA.

THE LOSS OF THE SEPARATE CLERK'S FEE

One of the key symbols of professional status is that a professional is
hired for a fee, not employed at a salary. Barristers' clerks have
always jealously guarded their fee. The case of Lyster *v*. Spearman in
1882 established the right to it once the barrister had been paid.[23]
Since then the BCA has successfully resisted all attacks on the clerk's

fee. In 1967 it was pleased to see in a report of the Joint Committee of
the General Council of the Bar and the Council of the Law Society:

The question has been discussed as to whether the existing practice of the
client being required to pay additional fees to barristers' clerks should be
discontinued . . . The Joint Committee are agreed that a change in this
traditional practice would confer no advantage on the public . . . We are sure
our members will consider that this is a very satisfactory situation, and it is
to be hoped that the long protracted criticism and argument against clerks'
fees is now at an end and can be considered closed for the foreseeable future.
[AR, 1867: 2–3]

Unfortunately the 'foreseeable future' came to an end sooner than
expected. The decimalisation Act of 1967 proposed that the currency
should change in 1971. In 1969 the Bar Council set up the Monroe
committee to examine the problems. The BCA recommended that
the clerk's fee should remain *sui generis*. The Bar saw decimalisation
as an opportunity to rationalise the system of counsel's fees. The
central idea was to incorporate the barrister's and clerk's fees into one
lump sum, and allocate a proportion to the clerk. According to one
of the BCA negotiators, the representatives of the Bar Council were
'stunned into silence' by the clerks' refusal to sacrifice their fees.
Nevertheless at an extraordinary meeting of the BCA the 'Members
[showed] that they [were] not adverse to the proposals of the Bar
Council . . .' (AR, 1969: 3). The traditionalists on the management
committee, however, believed that such a radical change in the
structure of the clerk's fee would destroy the independence of the
barrister's clerk.

In January 1970 the matter was concluded when the clerks agreed
to a formula whereby five per cent of the brief fee would be the
clerk's as of right. This was equivalent to an average of the old High
Court scale fees. However, the figure of five per cent was not easily
arrived at. Some members of the Bar Council thought half that
would be fairer. But the clerks argued that simply calculating
percentages from the scale fees excluded the off-scale fees for such
work as conferences which was charged at a higher rate. A further
percentage, up to five per cent, was to be negotiated between
barrister and clerk. Thus a clerk *could* receive ten per cent of the brief
fee.

The agreement was reported in the BCA's annual report for 1970
and in the Bar Council's annual statement for 1969–70. It was then
that a slight but important difference was noticed between the two.

The problem of the moving apostrophe had arisen. The clerks'
report stated: 'This arrangement of 5% covers only the *"clerk's fee"*
content of the fee' (AR, 1970: 2; emphasis added), whereas the Bar
Council report recorded: 'When any fee is thus quoted and
subsequently received as a single fee, 5% of that fee shall be received
and dealt with on the same terms as have hitherto applied to *"clerks'
fees"* (emphasis added).[24] Moreover, a member of the BCA
management committee pointed out, the original wording agreed
between the Council and the BCA was 'that 5% of the composite fee
shall be the clerk's in any event'; but the Bar had misprinted it. The
difference in the position of the apostrophe meant that in the BCA
version only the senior clerk would receive the commission,
whereas the Bar Council version could be interpreted to mean that
all the clerks in the chambers would share the commission.

The clerks' fears were intensified when a rumour circulated that
the Bar might use its version as a bargaining counter to force them
into accepting a percentage commission based on a barrister's net
(gross fees less expenses) rather than gross fees. They believed that
barristers would inflate their expenses. In exchange for this shift in
accounting practice, the Bar would agree to the BCA version of the
apostrophe. Although the moving apostrophe has not yet been used
against clerks—their commission is still calculated on gross
fees—the BCA is aware that some of its members are worried by the
possibility. Perhaps they should be, for in its evidence to the Royal
Commission on Legal Services the Bar said:

The Senate and the Barristers' Clerks' Association are discussing the
possibility of altering the basis of the senior clerk's remuneration so that:
(a) subject to the 5% agreement (see A.17.4) which is also under discussion,
    it does not increase in direct ratio to the increase in the size of the
    chambers; and
(b) it bears a reasonable ratio to and is directly or indirectly related to the net
    fees of his principals rather than their gross fees before deducting
    professional expenses.[25]

At present the influences determining the clerk's fee are in a state of
flux.[26]

CONCLUSION

Throughout its documented history the BCA has tried to extend its
authority over clerks, by disciplinary control and by seeking a closed
shop, by raising the educational threshold for entry, and by claiming

business efficiency expertise. Its success has been limited. But one important, though perhaps unintended, consequence of its ambitions is that it has provided a means by which the Bar can transmit decisions affecting all barristers' clerks.

The BCA negotiates with the Bar and other bodies, though not all clerks belong to it.[27] There is general apathy towards it among clerks. They are prepared to attend general meetings, but little more. When the BCA circulated a questionnaire on remuneration in order to prepare evidence for the Royal Commission on Legal Services, the response rate was too low to be useful. The older clerks, those over thirty-five, were satisfied to leave the control of the association to those who were eager to organise it. Among the younger clerks there has been a growing dissatisfaction with its role. The criticism has been voiced that the BCA is interested only in preserving the *status quo* for the older members, that it is an organisation of the old guard, that it is not prepared to stand against the Bar, and that it has done little to discourage prejudice against ethnic minorities and female clerks.

The BCA has centred its campaign for professional status on the concept of the clerk's fee, but here too it has lost ground steadily. With the increase in the size of chambers the pressure is mounting from the Bar for clerks to take a reduction in their percentage commission. The BCA has been unable to resist. And the result of *ex parte* Cotton, that a clerk's fee is a mere gratuity, has indirectly been resurrected in the 1978 unfair dismissal case of Arthur Magraw, whose fight against a reduction in his commission resulted in dismissal and the decision that clerks are in fact self-employed.

NOTES

1   Not all of the minute books are in easily identifiable locations. Moreover the set of annual reports which I consulted was the only known set in existence. When the BCA was evicted from its room in the Law Courts a large number of documents and records were thrown away by the court staff and never recovered.

2   There were typed reports for the years 1938–49, but these have been lost.

3   But Lord Evershed did comment, 'I cannot quite help feeling that if a particular Counsel's Clerk has marked his Principal's brief with Ten Thousand Guineas one day and is then asked to accept a brief in which the right fee may be Fifty or Sixty Guineas, he begins to lose all sense of reality; Fifty or Sixty Guineas means nothing at all.' (P.R.O., L.C.O. 2, Pieces 4030–5.)

4 According to a member of the BCA management committee, the three chambers folded up within a year.

5 Benson (1979: I, para. 34.27) also noted that barristers' clerks' pensions are grossly inadequate and that the Senate should help to improve the situation.

6 526 Parl. Deb. H.C. (5th ser.), col. 1893 (1954).

7 526 Parl. Deb. H.C. (5th ser.), col. 1893 (1954).

8 Sir Frank Soskice, 526 Parl. Deb. H.C. (5th ser.), col. 1898 (1954).

9 526 Parl. Deb. H.C. (5th ser.), col. 1901 (1954).

10 526 Parl. Deb. H.C. (5th ser.), col. 1901 (1954).

11 The Judges' Clerks' Association has usually been managed by the ex-barrister's clerk contingent.

12 See Abel-Smith and Stevens (1967: 426–33; 1968: 119).

13 Previous careers of judge's clerks (from the Lord Chancellor's Office, personal communication, 1977): barrister's clerk, thirty; solicitor's clerk, three; Royal Navy, twelve; army, thirteen; RAF, three; police, nineteen; miscellaneous, twelve. In a communication from the Lord Chancellor's Office (1981) I was informed that 'Few, if any, are ex-barristers' clerks.'

14 *The Times*, 10 December 1959.

15 *The Times*, 15 December 1959.

16 See Zander (1968: 88–90) and *Sunday Times*, 23 May 1965.

17 *Sunday Times*, 3 November 1968. Also see chapter 3 and appendix 1.

18 See Michael Zander, *Guardian*, 13 February 1976.

19 See Boulton (1975: 52n) and the Senate (1980: para. 5 (a)).

20 See chapter 2.

21 During my own observations I found little trace of the manual; if there was one, it was usually to be found in the bottom of a drawer under a pile of papers. Some clerks had never seen it. They would look at my copy, only to hand it back with a derisory comment.

22 See Rodney Voyce, 'Computers in barristers' chambers', *Law Society's Gazette*, 25 November 1981: 1333.

23 Judge Bayley remarked that 'it was well known that fees paid to a barrister included fees to which the clerk was beyond all doubt entitled'. Lyster *v*. Spearman (1882), 72 L.T. Jo. 391; 3 Digest (Repl.) 360. But the Master of the Rolls disagreed in *ex parte* Cotton, where he said, 'the [clerk's] fee is, in its legal character, a mere gratuity, a favour, indeed, for which attention and civility are reasonably expected in return, but for which there is no legal demand'. (1846) 9 Beav. 107, 115. The Master of the Rolls appears to have found inspiration in the following note appended to the report: 'Neither do our learned men of the law grow to good estates in the commonwealth by any illiberal means, (as envie sometimes suggesteth), but in a most ingenious and worthy manner. For the fees or rewards which they receive are not of the nature of wages or pay, or that we call salary or hire, which are indeed duties certain and grow due by contract for labour or service, but that which is given to a learned councellor is called *honorarium* and not *merces*, being indeed a gift which giveth honour as well to the taker as to the giver: neither is it certain or contracted, for no price or rate can

be set upon councel which is unvaluable and inestimable, so as it is more or less, according to circumstances, viz the ability of the client, the worthiness of the councellor, the weightiness of the cause, and the custom of the country. Briefly, it is a gift of such a nature, and given and taken upon such terms, as albeit the able client may not neglect to give it without note of ingratitude, (for it is but a gratuity or token of thankfulness), yet the worthy councellor may not demand it without doing wrong to his reputation, according to that moral rule, *"multa honeste accipi possunt, quae tamen honeste peti non possunt"*.' ((1846) 9 Beav. 107, 116.)

24 Annual Statement of the General Council of the Bar (1969–70: 33).

25 Senate evidence to the Royal Commission on Legal Services, Section III, A.20.1.

26 Cf. the case of Mr Arthur Magraw, chapter 1.

27 For example, in 1966, when the Bar Council was discussing the abrogation of the two-thirds rule (stating that a junior barrister should automatically receive a fee equal to two-thirds of the leader's fee), the BCA made known its views to the Bar Council as follows: 'The subject of the 2/3rds rule has been fully canvassed amongst our members and, subsequent to a Special Meeting of the Association . . . over 200 Clerks recorded their vote on suggested changes in the rule. More than 85% were in favour of retaining the 2/3rds rule in its present form, but, in the event of a change being thought necessary, approximately the same percentage of Clerks were in favour of alternative 'A' in the Bar Council's Memorandum . . . namely a reduction in the ceiling to which the rule should operate. The result of this ballot, as reported to the Council, clearly showed an overwhelming majority against the abrogation of the rule in its entirety.

'The operation of the present rule, and the substituted rule of "free negotiation" are and will be part of the Clerk's duties in dealing with fees and our experience is such that we believe that the substituted rule will not only be difficult or impossible to work but will result in a serious diminution in Counsel's fees . . .

'As regards Legal Aid fees, which . . . it is intended should be assessed on the same basis as ordinary fees, namely as if the junior had been briefed alone, we consider with respect is even more unsatisfactory. Legal Aid fees cannot be negotiated whether the rule is changed or not, and whereas at the present time Legal Aid fees conform to the 2/3rds rule (without a ceiling) when such rule goes the assessment of the hypothetical fee will be completely at large . . .

'We also consider that without the yardstick of the present, or a reduced, 2/3rds rule fees of junior Counsel will tend to become a 'free for all'. Solicitors will be failing in their duty to their client not to shop around to find the Counsel who will take the lowest fee when briefed with a leader, and will be committing no breach of etiquette in so doing. Similarly Counsel's Clerk will be anxious to do the best they can for their Principal, and who can say whether the fee "freely negotiated" in such circumstances is either undercutting or improper.'

Chapter 8
CONCLUSION

In a lecture to young barristers' clerks the secretary of the Barristers' Clerks' Association said, 'the barrister's Senior Clerk is in a sense, separately employed by each barrister, and also in a sense, not employed by any' (Cooper, n.d.: 10). To those outside the legal profession, and to many of those within it, such a description must appear puzzling and contradictory. But the clerk occupies just such a no-man's-land in the English legal system. And yet the present structure relies heavily on the clerk for his knowledge of listing procedures, fee-fixing, and his capacity for dealing with the personnel of the legal profession. The by-ways and labyrinths of the law are the essence of the clerk's work. And among clerks there is a strong desire to preserve this situation. The concept of the clerk's fee assists them in this: a fee connotes a distance between the practitioner and the client—but who, in this case, is the client?

In one sense, all those the clerk encounters in his everyday routine are his clients—his barristers, his solicitors, the list officers, and occasionally the lay client. The clerk is a broker, though not entirely a free agent. His primary loyalty must be to his barristers. But, besides providing counsel, he is valued for his ability to liaise with the courts and other barristers' clerks who may be involved in the cases. His brokerage activities are not always immediately rewarded. Sometimes the reward takes the form of favours instead of cash. The ability to call on a favour owed may be more important in a crisis (for example, over a clash of court dates) than money.

Not all the clerks' clients find it easy to accept this ambiguous role. The Law Society said in its evidence to the Royal Commission on Legal Services that clerks were overoptimistic about the amount of work that their barristers could accomplish and about the chances of cases settling.[1] The society believed that this optimism was encouraged by the clerk's commission. Instead of negotiations being conducted through the clerk it preferred the alternative of solicitors dealing direct with barristers, especially regarding fees.

The Bar, too, is unhappy, mainly about the dramatic rise in clerks' incomes caused by the growth in the size of chambers. It wants clerks to change from taking a percentage of gross fees to using net fees as the baseline. Another effect of the growth in the size of chambers has been a marked reluctance by clerks to take on smaller, less well established sets. The clerk's entrepreneurial role has been diminished in these larger chambers. In its place the administrative function has assumed greater importance. Little touting is needed to attract and keep the business of the solicitors who use the larger chambers. The relationship is similar to two law firms working together. In such a system the clerk's place would be assumed by an office manager trained in legal procedure, conversant with modern communications systems and skilled in proper accounting procedures. Most probably such a manager would earn a high salary and possibly enjoy partnership prospects.

Most clerks' expertise in this direction derives from experience. Hardly any thought or sustained research designed to remedy deficiencies has been carried out by the Bar. The BCA's efforts at improving business management have had but slight impact.

Unfortunately the Royal Commission on Legal Services did not come up with a fundamental reappraisal of the position of the barrister's clerk. The impression it gave was that any problem on this score was essentially an internal matter for the Bar. The commission did recommend the abolition of the rule that a barrister must have the services of a clerk in order to practise. Some form of secretarial assistance was thought necessary, but the commission did not feel that it had to be provided by the traditional type of clerk (Benson 1979: I, para. 34.7). On the question of fees, the commission recommended a salary as a preferable alternative to the percentage (Benson 1979: I, para. 34.26). High pressure of work could be rewarded by a system of bonus payments.

The big increase in work for the Bar has been in criminal law. Most of the fees in criminal work are paid by legal aid. Indeed, the junior Bar receives fifty per cent of its income from public funds; hence so do clerks.[2] Members of the legal profession, and clerks, have at times expressed low regard for legally aided clients.[3] But the rise in legally aided work has meant, paradoxically, less work for the clerk. Fees are not discussed, if at all, until after the event, and much of the work is just bookkeeping for the legal aid authority.

Some of the older guard have felt dismay at the changes in the Bar and, concomitantly, in the style of clerking. Aylett, talking about his final years of clerking in 1971, said:

Numbers [of barristers] too had got out of hand . . . Legal Aid had transformed the economics of the profession . . . Accompanying Legal Aid was the rise in the crime rate, and in the numbers of petitions for divorce. The traditional type of work of our chambers had also changed, and the speed with which it was disposed of was faster; cases merely became book entries. So many of the old subtleties used by a chief clerk were no longer required . . . My 'mistress' had grown obese and was wearing ill-fitting clothes. There were too many new laws, too many lawyers, too many courts and judges. I felt with Quintin [Hogg], when he had said that barristers should be few, of unblemished character and highly qualified. [1978: 159]

Why, then, do barristers' clerks exist? The answer is probably that they serve a useful function for the Bar. That function is to act as 'gatekeeper', or filter. A filter is necessary because the Bar considers itself an open, meritocratic occupation. The claim notwithstanding, it has remained notably small and select throughout its history. Gatekeeping was usually unnecessary: class alone was a sufficient barrier. This is perhaps shown by a statement attributed to Quintin Hogg by his clerk, Aylett: 'The solicitor is a man of business, a barrister an artist and a scholar' (1978: 160). With the increase in educational opportunities since the second world war, class ceased to be an effective means of exclusion. In addition, the rise in legal aid work has assisted many junior barristers in the early stages of their careers. However, the Bar's refusal to extend its physical limits beyond the Inns of Court in London has remained a powerful deterrent to expansion. So too has the cost of pupilage.

The remainder of the filtering process is assigned to the clerk. His input in decisions about admitting new members is important. Often he will have been the only person to have spent any time observing the potential tenant during pupilage, especially in the second six months when the pupil is allowed to work. Indeed, it will have been the clerk who gave the pupil the chance to work. He may therefore be the only one in the chambers qualified, however dubiously, to judge the standard of the applicant. In most cases the clerk's criteria accord with those of the Bar, with a strong reluctance to accept women and members of ethnic minorities as tenants in chambers.

In their gatekeeping role clerks have esentially three choices: they can grant entry, refer the applicant to other chambers (as Bert and Arthur did in chapter 6) or refuse entry. A barrister must have the services of a clerk if he or she wants to practise, and will be dependent on those services for the first few years. This particular function of the barrister's clerk allows the Bar to make its claim of openness without having to substantiate it. Everett C. Hughes coined an apt phrase when he referred to 'good people and dirty work' (1971). The Bar maintains clean hands while the clerks do its dirty work. Clerks have been allowed to exploit a situation that redounds greatly to their benefit and that of the Bar.

The clerk has other useful functions. As long as the Bar forbids advertising, the clerk will be required to publicise the barrister. As long as the myth of the cab-rank rule is perpetuated, the barrister will need the clerk to turn away unwanted work. And as long as barristers want to join the lists of prosecutors they will need the clerk to help them. Barristers have abdicated a considerable degree of responsibility over their professional lives in favour of the clerk's control. If they suffer as a result they have only themselves to blame: for too long the Bar has clung to tradition.[4] It has sacrificed efficiency and merit in order to prevent many potential recruits from taking up a career in the law. Clerks are instruments, but important ones, in this process. Increased flexibility in the organisation of the Bar, such as allowing partnerships between barristers and with others, would alleviate many of the problems. A greater involvement by individual barristers in the planning of their careers would, in part, diminish the power of the clerk over career timetables and reduce the uncertainty of the early years of practice.

Whither clerks now?

NOTES

1 Law Society memorandum of evidence submitted to the Royal Commission on Legal Services, No. 3, Part 3, Section xiv. 6, 4.
2 Benson (1979: I, table 36.3).
3 See, for example, Lord Goddard's foreword in Daniell (1971), where he deplores the growth of legal aid.
4 Younger members of the Bar are, however, beginning to challenge its orthodoxy. See the essays in Hazell (1978c), the evidence of the Wellington Street chambers, and the journal *Legal Action Group Bulletin*.

Appendix 1

BIOGRAPHY OF A RESEARCH PROJECT

I do not know of any other study of the legal profession that has been carried out in the fashion of this one. Lawyers, by tradition, rarely step into the quagmire of fieldwork. Llewellyn spent only ten days in the field when he and Hoebel studied the Cheyenne (Twining, 1973): he preferred to work at his desk while Hoebel immersed himself in the quagmire. This account will, I hope, serve to illustrate some of the hazards and risks that a researcher has to contend with during the process of empirical and ethnographic research.[1]

I undertook the research for a graduate degree in socio-legal studies at the School of Law in the University of Warwick. My choice of topic emerged from my interest in the legal profession and legal culture.

The beginning. My search through literary sources did not prove of much benefit, because so little had been written about barristers' clerks. Those who had taken an interest in them, such as Zander (1968), Johnstone and Hopson (1967) and Abel-Smith and Stevens (1967, 1968), provided little or no information on how they acquired their data.

I checked biographies of lawyers and judges, but that type of memoir concentrates on the cases of, rather than the life of, the lawyer. Luckily, one of my supervisors discovered an autobiography of a barrister's clerk (Bowker, 1947; see also Bowker, 1961, and Aylett, 1978) which gave a colourful impression of legal life in the 1920s and 1930s. This book gave me some information about clerks on which to base my early investigations.

Few official sources mentioned barristers' clerks.[2] For example, the Beeching Commission on Assizes and Quarter Sessions (1969) received evidence from a large number of parties involved with the administration and use of the courts except, curiously, barristers' clerks. In answer to the question 'Why not?' the Lord Chancellor's Office said:

On reflection, I rather share your sense of surprise that the Beeching Report contains nothing about the part played by barristers' clerks in the administration of the system and, in particular, in making best use of barristers' time. I can assure you that the Royal Commission had their role very much in mind, and you will see a passing reference to this in evidence quoted at the end of paragraph 81 of the Report.[3]

Paragraph 81 contained an extract of the evidence submitted by the Clerk of

Assize for the North-eastern Circuit criticising the inefficiency of the peripatetic Assizes:

[The arguments] are levelled at the [Assize] system (if it can be called a system) which by its nature prevents an orderly pattern from ever emerging. The consequences are that solicitors, witnesses and others never know when they may be required, and barristers' clerks quite rightly take advantage of the lack of organisation to further their own ends. [Beeching, 1969: para. 81]

A reading of the Monopolies Commission report on professional services (1970), however, produced an interesting strand of enquiry. In the appendix to the report, comparisons were drawn between the Bars of England, Scotland and Northern Ireland. Of these, only the English Bar had adopted the chambers system. The other two appeared to manage not only without chambers but also without clerks. Attracted by the idea of including a comparative aspect, I wrote to the Secretary of the Northern Ireland Bar Council but received no reply. Obtaining information from the Faculty of Advocates in Edinburgh, however, was more problematic still, because of the cultural separation between the Scottish and the English, especially in the legal professions. My supervisor, through his professional contacts, discovered to whom I should write: 'the Clerk to the Faculty of Advocates'. And here I made a blunder. I misinterpreted the title, thinking it, perhaps, to be a Scottish equivalent to the English barrister's clerk, which was curious in the light of the Monopolies Commission report's statement that none existed. I wrote enquiring about the pattern of the clerk's career and so forth in Scotland and was answered in no uncertain terms:

I was interested to hear of your research . . . and have little doubt that comparison with the profession in other countries might be interesting to you. I think, however, it is of the first importance that you should appreciate that the Scottish legal system is separate, distinct, and in no sense a variant of the English legal system. The proper method of studying it is to assume that it is different until you have received information to suggest that it is the same. While there are obvious identities in the substantive law, there is almost no similarity in matters of procedure and organisation of the profession. If you think of Scotland merely as a variant you will err exceedingly and wholly misunderstand the position.

. . . You enquire 'what services do you provide for the members of the Faculty', but as this comes at the end of a sentence concerning Advocates' Clerks perhaps I should explain first that I am not an Advocate's Clerk. The use of similar titles may be confusing. The Faculty has five annually elected officers, elected from amongst the practising Advocates, and I am one of these. As Clerk of Faculty, or, in English, Honorary Secretary of the Scottish Bar, I am responsible for the day to day management . . .[4]

Thus I learned to be somewhat more cautious when delving into areas where my ignorance was total.

The only productive official source was the 1953 report on Supreme Court practice (Evershed, 1953), in which evidence had been taken from barristers' clerks.

During this preliminary stage certain criticisms were aimed at my proposal of doing a field study of barristers' clerks. The main one was that I might be denied the access necessary for success. As an alternative I could couch the research in terms of the theory of professionalism and professionalisation. I was reluctant to follow this course, but I realised the necessity of contingency measures and started my reading in the subject.[5]

Access plans. It may sound a simple question, but how was I to reach the clerks? That is, I knew barristers' clerks were situated in the same area as barristers, but I did not know whom to contact.

Most occupational groups, especially those in the professional stratum, are represented by some form of association or body. I was aware that the barristers' clerks had formed one, as Abel-Smith and Stevens acknowledged the assistance given by the Barristers' Clerks' Association and, moreover, referred to its annual reports.[6] One possible solution would have been to ask the Senate of the Inns of Court and Bar. I resisted this line of attack because I thought I should try to avoid being 'contaminated' by any connection with the Bar. Instead I sent enquiries to two legal journals, the *Law Society Gazette* and the *New Law Journal* and to Professor Abel-Smith at the London School of Economics. The editor of the *Gazette* replied, giving me the name and address of the Barristers' Clerks' Association's secretary and telling me, 'I have already spoken to him about your letter and he is prepared to give you any information and help he can.' I now felt that my approach would no longer be a totally 'cold canvass'. Abel-Smith, on the other hand, in answer to my queries about the location and value of the BCA annual reports that were untraceable in any library, could not remember much about the material and suggested that the BCA had changed its name to the Legal Executives' Association. Barristers' clerks had certainly not changed their name, and 'legal executives' is the term now used by those who were formerly referred to as solicitors' managing clerks.

Breaking in. It was now time to enter the field; I had exhausted all other possible sources. I drafted a letter to the Secretary of the Barristers' Clerks' Association in which, among other things, I said:

I have been studying the literature on the legal profession and it appears to me that too much attention has been paid to barristers and solicitors. I wish to shift the emphasis to professions like your own, especially as they are such an important part of the legal profession. One often receives an incomplete picture of the legal profession because of this, and so I would like to redress the balance and complete the picture.

I also included a few questions on numbers of barristers' clerks, recruitment difficulties, training, etc. Nothing contentious was mentioned at this stage.

While waiting for a reply I began to devise a schedule of questions on basic socio-demographic matters and professionalism, which could be adapted into either a mailed questionnaire or an interview format. The latter seemed more likely, for, as one of my supervisors put it, 'clerks see themselves as on a par with Queen's Counsel'.

In addition I discussed the project with Senior Master Jacob of the Queen's Bench Division, whose son had taught me at the London School of Economics. Although primarily a practitioner, he maintained a substantial interest in the academic aspects of law and procedure. He commented:

I think you have chosen a very interesting, important and somewhat neglected subject, namely the role of what you call the unadmitted personnel who form part of the English Legal System, which is sometimes for short called 'paralegal' personnel. Very little has been done about this subject and it would be very useful for the profession as a whole and indeed the general public to know a great deal more of how the legal profession operates on these levels, which is really of fundamental importance, to the work that they do.[7]

After some weeks the Secretary of the Barristers' Clerks' Association wrote offering to discuss the purpose of my research with me. The break had finally come.

The prospect of meeting a barrister's clerk made me quite nervous, so I took meticulous care over my preparation. Linked with these preparations was the interview with Senior Master Jacob, who, recognising his influence in the legal community, allowed me to use his name as a lever in order to secure co-operation.

My preparations involved both positive and negative features. On the negative side I had decided that my association with Michael Zander and the London School of Economics should remain hidden to avoid presenting, however unintentionally, any witch-hunting impressions.[8] On the positive side, I created a respectable outward appearance. I believe this to be of the utmost importance, and Stone (1962) confirms my beliefs:

Appearance *substitutes* for past and present action and, at the same time, conveys an *incipience* permitting others to anticipate what is about to occur. Specifically, clothing represents our action, past, present, and future, as it is established by the proposals and anticipations that occur in every social transaction. [Stone, 1962: 100]

Moreover:

By appearing, the person *announces* his identity, *shows* his value, *expresses* his mood, or *proposes* his attitude . . . In other words, when one's dress calls out in others the 'same' identification of the wearer as it calls out in the wearer, we may speak of the appearance as meaningful. [Stone, 1962: 101]

So I cut my hair to collar length, and because I could not afford a suit, compromised by buying a jacket, trousers and tie. I thought it sensible not to appear too similar to a clerk but definitely to remove myself as far as possible from the stereotype of a student. Subsequently a clerk told me that my dress resembled that of a clerk in court vacation clothes.

I had never visited a barristers' chambers before. It was all strange. The chambers' entrance had two doors, an inner and an outer. A list of the occupants' names was painted on the outer door. Once through, however, I found myself in a long, book-lined corridor where I could hear voices coming from the clerks' room. I introduced myself to the clerks, who were all junior clerks, and was asked to wait in the corridor. The senior clerk kept me waiting for just over half an hour before he came out of his room.

'Hello, Mr Flood. I'm sorry to have kept you waiting for so long. Do come in.'

'Oh . . . that's quite all right.'

'Well, I've got your letter. What can I do for you?'

I explain I want to write about the neglected aspects of the legal profession.

'Mmm, but why barristers' clerks?'

I further explain that, believing the clerk to be of considerable importance in the legal system, I think a detailed, objective picture of the clerk should be drawn.

'Yes, well, we need a serious study of our part of the profession. I myself have done some work. Each year I give some lectures to the young clerks in the Temple on the etiquette of the Bar, and in the past (it's been dropped now) I would preface my remarks with some of the history of the clerks. There isn't much, but I'm still looking. You know Michael Zander did his research here?'

'No?'

'Yes, he spent a couple of days in my clerks' room. Of course, he got it all wrong. Zander suppressed the truth and deliberately distorted what took place. Look . . .' He showed me a passage from Zander's book (1968: 86): 'The clerk sits at the fountain and can control the direction of the spray' (i.e. the distribution of work among the barristers). 'Now what really happens is this. We have two diaries, one for the senior men in chambers—see, their names are in order of call, and they're all booked up for weeks in advance. I can't move their work around. This other diary is for what I call the "tupenny-ha'penny work". These are all the junior members of chambers, and most of them work from day to day, so I like to keep their days filled. *This* is the only type of work I can transfer from one member of chambers to another—the returns—because it comes into chambers at such short notice. There are times when it goes wrong. Mr X. was asked to chair an enquiry which was supposed to last only ten days: it eventually stretched to seventy days, so I had to return a lot of his work . . . I started in the Temple as a boy before the war. I had to make the tea, carry the coal up three floors from the cellar, and gradually I was given more responsibility.'

He consented to tackle my questionnaire and arrange some interviews and let me know the results in due course. He was very generous with his time—he gave me nearly an hour. His manner and the style of his room (antique desk) bespoke considerable self-esteem and awareness of his own importance. The image was a little tarnished, however, by the presence of the photocopying machine. My impression formed along the lines that he was not taking me quite as seriously as I had hoped.[9]

Then I had a stroke of good fortune which radically altered the design of the project. During a talk a friend told me that he was on friendly terms with a first junior clerk of a chambers that was used by the neighbourhood law centre he worked for. He thought this clerk would probably allow me to interview him. Within the next five minutes he had telephoned and arranged an interview for the next morning.

'Gordon', the junior clerk, brought clerking alive for me. He conveyed the sense of urgency and tension that was inherent in the job. And he projected an idea of the cameraderie between clerks.

'How would you describe the relationship between members of chambers and yourself?'

'It's a love–hate relationship. We need each other, but they can make my job hard. Like, we have a rule in chambers that every member must phone in at least twice a day in case we've got a brief that needs doing urgently. Right, we've got a couple of barristers who haven't been phoning in as they should and we've been losing work. Well, George' (the senior clerk) 'has had a go at them, but it didn't do no good. One of them thought that *he* could decide when he wanted to phone in. In the end George had to complain to the head of chambers, and it was brought up at the last chambers meeting we had. Yeah, and now they're phoning in every morning and every afternoon . . .

'We tell pupils to keep quiet, watch their pupil masters, keep out of the clerks' room, and not to use the telephone, or he'll give himself a bad name . . .

'The busiest time of day for us is between 4 p.m. and 6.30 p.m.: the phones go beserk. George sits there talking into four phones at once; he's amazing. You can't tell what it's like unless you see it. It's impossible to describe. Afterwards I go for a drink with the lads.'

'Since you mentioned that I should see it in order to understand what it's like in the afternoon, do you think it might be possible for me to spend a day with you in the clerks' room just watching what goes on?'

Gordon agreed to ask his senior clerk about my request, but I was not optimistic. My friend had warned me that Gordon would speak to me but definitely would not have me in as an observer. Certainly I did hope he would agree, as a day's observation, I believed, would enliven the interview data.

When I subsequently telephoned to find out the decision I was answered by Gordon's senior clerk. I was suddenly in an awkward position. Should I act as though he knew of me? Should I ring off and try again until I got Gordon? Had Gordon in fact said anything to him? I tried to play safe, and asked to speak to Gordon. The senior clerk did not pass me over immediately but had a whispered conversation with Gordon. Then he returned to me, and, in an extremely abrupt tone, said, 'I think it's *me* you want to speak to. If you wish to seek permission to enter my chambers you must ask me. *I am the senior clerk.*'

I apologised profusely; then he asked me how long I would want to stay. When I suggested two or three days so I could become acquainted with the procedures of the clerks' room, he was reluctant.

'Oh, I don't know about that . . . it's a bit long, we'll have to see.' He asked me to give him a few days' notice before I wanted to come.

To digress for a moment: because this was my first research project I felt extremely anxious about its success, especially as so many variables were beyond my control. At times my doubts brought me to the stage where I wished I had taken up a piece of 'safe' library research. But what became increasingly frustrating was the discrepancy between the progress of my research and the conventional accounts of research which gave the impression of having proceeded with 'ne'er a single hitch'. With this in mind I began reflecting on the irony of the fact that the most substantial piece of research anyone does is generally undertaken at the lowest level of research experience. Although it is true that this type of experience is meant to provide a training, the magnitude of its influence is such that one's whole future career can hinge on the success or failure of that particular project. Nevertheless I was commited to my study.

But my hitches were these: first, mistaking the proper identity of the clerk to the Faculty of Advocates, a minor blunder; second, my awkwardness over the telephone to the senior clerk; the third, however, was completely unexpected, and it almost sounded the death knell for the entire project and also multiplied my anxieties beyond measure.

I telephoned the chambers to submit a firm date for my visit. I was careful to ask for the senior clerk. He enquired whether I had read the *New Statesman* that day. I told him I had not. He then launched into a lengthy tirade against an article entitled 'NCOs of the law.' There was one paragraph, in particular, that had greatly upset him.

One person who felt the clerks' prejudice is a clerk herself: Mary Hickson, the clerk of the most unusual chambers in Britain, those of Lord Gifford in Lambeth. She works in an office that has a notice 'Sue the Bastards!' by the door and an anti-anti-abortion poster in the window. As part of her training for clerking, she spent two months in 'The Cloisters' . . . 'I learned how much I disliked the Temple and how much they don't want a woman to be a clerk. The senior clerk there just told me to go away and get married.' This prejudice is exercised against women as barristers, though, says Hickson, 'they think they're okay for some things like matrimonial work.' [Bugler, 1976: 286]

In addition the article referred to the criticism that the barrister's clerk's commission tended to inflate the fees charged to clients.

The senior clerk vehemently denied that clerks were biased against women; he even said that when a new set of chambers was being established he had recommended a woman as clerk. The description of the clerks' room, including its posters, represented to him a gross violation of good taste and proper conduct. 'I certainly wouldn't have posters and a sign saying "Sue the bastards!" in my clerks' room.' He also felt that clerks were being unjustifiably attacked over the question of counsel's fees and put forward the defence that certain occasions and circumstances demanded he reduce or even waive some fees. Sometimes, he said, the fault lay with solicitors, who offered unneccessarily high fees to counsel: for example, one solicitor suggested a £50 fee for a matrimonial matter that, at best was worth only £25.

The upshot was, however, that no barrister's clerk would allow me, or any other researcher, to enter their chambers—a total, eternal ban. I felt dizzy with shock, but my reflexes took over and for the following twenty minutes

I virtually pleaded with him to change his mind. I pointed out the advantages, in that I would be able to present a fair and objective picture of clerking, which would naturally suffer through my not having experienced the urgency and frenzy of the clerks' room. And, as a final argument. I offered him the opportunity to read and criticise my writing, but without assigning any editorial control to him. To my surprise, and relief, the arguments had some effect. He began to retreat from his position and question me about the length of my stay. I answered that two or three days would be sufficient (bearing in mind his previous objections). Again he raised objections but, greatly to my surprise, now considered it short and instead suggested I extend the visit to a week, when he could take me to the Old Bailey and the Law Courts. Paradoxically my situation had actually improved as a result of this apparent catastrophe. It was as though he wanted me to prove the article false.

My intention was to spend a short time in the chambers and then return to the secretary of the Barristers' Clerks' Association to carry out the interviews. In short, the stint of participant observation would supplement the interview data.

In the field. The senior clerk suggested I arrive at his chambers at about 10 a.m. (even though he arrived at 9.30 a.m.), because 'nothing happens before then.' When I walked into the chambers it was obvious he had forgotten who I was. But after a few moments he recognised me and introduced me to his colleagues.

The chambers was a common law set. That is, between them, the barristers could tackle most legal problems except the more esoteric areas such as patent and tax law. There were more than twenty tenants (i.e. members of the chambers), about six pupil barristers who could work, and three pupils in their first six months of pupilage. The staff consisted of the senior clerk, the first junior, the second junior, a typist and a part-time accounts clerk. All, except the accounts clerk, occupied the same room. It had been designed to suit the needs of the clerk, and consequently there was no truly convenient place for me.

All the clerks' tools and materials were immediately at hand. The senior and first junior clerks sat opposite each other, with a trough between them which contained the solicitor clients' ledgers. Resting on top of them were two large red diaries—one for the senior barristers, the other for the juniors—which were constantly passed between the two clerks during the day. Each clerk had three telephones, the most important instrument in the chambers. Behind the first junior clerk were stacked the barristers' trays in which mail and briefs awaited collection. Hence every barrister was, in effect, forced to pass through the clerks' room every time he entered or left the chambers to check the inflow of work—so enabling the clerks to monitor their barristers' movements.

I was placed next to the senior clerk, who gave me some papers, letters and fee notes to browse through while he worked. Since I did not want to interrupt his routine too frequently, I tried to be as unobtrusive as possible. I just sat with a notebook, recording conversations, answers to questions, people's movements, and my impressions. No one commented on the presence of the notebook. But in one respect I need not have worried, as the clerks did not appear overburdened by their work.

The first two days in this set of chambers were, in retrospect the most crucial I spent in the field. During this period I realised that my project would have to undergo a fundamental alteration in focus and method, from a study based on the sociology of professions to one of ethnography and fieldwork. The clerks' behaviour showed an intention to demonstrate that clerking was an esoteric practice and an honourable calling. They were keen to show me the better side of their craft, but their actions, I believe, went beyond mere showmanship. There was a genuine concern that I should learn; in contrast to the Secretary of the BCA, they took me seriously. And by the end of the second day in the Temple I had been introduced to George's friends, who were tentatively prepared to support the research by accepting me into their chambers.

The decision to make this change in the research was intuitive. I 'knew' I was going to be able to implement the scheme of research I had originally intended—a field research study of barristers' clerks without the hindrance, as I saw it, of the sociology of the professions. But one consequence was a strong sense of having been left in limbo. The successful introduction and friendly relations with the clerks gave me the confidence to attempt a field research study, but all my energies and thoughts had been directed toward interviews as the main sources of data. Hence the internal wranglings on how to succeed in field research, for, apart from reading a few monographs, I had had no training, and, worse, in order to seize the moment I did not have time to retreat from the field and learn the proper techniques, if any. As William F. Whyte (1955: 357) remarked, 'I did not develop [my] ideas by any strictly logical process. They dawned on me out of what I was seeing, hearing, doing—and feeling. They grew out of an effort to organise a confusing welter of experience.'

Over the next few months the pace at which my research progressed startled me, leaving me at times quite bewildered. With George, the first senior, as sponsor, my presence was being accepted. One clerk went as far as to joke that I would soon become an 'honorary clerk' (probably more of a joke against me than for me). The legitimation of my position was strongly assisted by George's status among the others. Within his own clique there was no doubt he was *primus inter pares,* and among clerks at large his reputation commanded respect and not a little envy. No one, therefore, was going to contradict explicitly his evaluation of me, but I was not to know the force of his influence until I moved to another set of chambers.

In all, I spent over a month at his chambers. He gave me a solid grounding in the features of the clerk's job. I was even given the opportunity to be his junior when his first junior took a holiday. Neither of us discussed my active participation in the clerks' room: it just emerged naturally, for with the sudden vacancy a pair of idle hands seemed incongruous. Through answering the telephone I became aware of the closely textured relationship between solicitor and clerk. The solicitor relied on the same voice coming over the telephone, thus ensuring the development of trust between them.

My answering could almost be interpreted as a betrayal of that trust. The voice they heard was foreign to them, and they would demand to know who I was or to be transferred to someone they knew.

The telephone, as I have already mentioned, is the most important tool the clerk possesses. And enormous significance is assigned to the recognition of the speaker's voice. This recognition of identity is a prerequisite of normal conversation, otherwise the natural sequences are interrupted and confusion results (cf. Garfinkel, 1967). One feature shared by many clerks is the cockney accent that points up their East End origins. One clerk has been moved to declare, 'One of the greatest attributes of counsel is his diction. We clerks should emulate them. Many of us were born cockneys, but it is not necessary to thrust this fact down everybody's ears' (Newland, 1971). My own accent is typically standard English—the same as many lawyers'. So, to explain away this irremediable incongruity, George would refer to me as a 'temporary trainee clerk', which usually satisfied the enquirer.

Through George my project was transformed. He showed me the courts, the pubs, and the cafés where clerks and lawyers hang out. I became associated with the Temple football team, of which he was manager and trainer. Besides familiarising me with the clerk's domain, he acquainted me with his opinions of other clerks, giving me a rough-and-ready scale by which to gauge them. One clerk, for instance, was considered 'a great person' to drink with but, unfortunately, he had a 'hopeless set' (and he drank too much), so George never passed him any work. Another was too harsh on his barristers; they needed kinder treatment. George, however, placed himself between these two categories—the ideal clerk.

In general, clerks do hold themselves in high esteem. They need to, in order to sell counsel to solicitors and fix fees and arrange court lists. But they do doubt themselves, especially their ability to hold their chambers together. And to assuage their doubts they would frequently speculate on possible or probable schisms in other sets. Much of this kind of introspective talk would come out during the hours spent in pubs.

While I was in George's chambers the Secretary of the BCA wrote to me. I had been waiting for him to complete my questionnaire. He wrote, 'I suddenly remembered you yesterday, and tried to find the questionnaire I was going to fill in for you—regretfully without success. Could you kindly send me another? . . . I don't know whether you saw the article in *The New Statesman*. I should be interested to hear your views.' Several clerks told me to have nothing to do with him, especially George, who said, 'Tell him I'm looking after you now.' I refused to sever all connection and did try to have him complete another questionnaire. But I felt more secure in not having to rely on the Secretary for all my access.

The next couple of sets I visited were clerked by friends of George. They were all common law chambers, generalist, but with a bias to criminal law, and I was becoming concerned that I might be restricted to this type because the circles I moved in were basically of this kind. But I did, if possible, want to explore other types, such as civil and Chancery.

The art of taking notes politely. In that first set of chambers my notebook was ever-present, and I recorded everything I possibly could in it. I filled page after page while sitting in the clerks' room—conversations, movements, people and so forth. However, there were situations when I had to abandon it. I could not, for example, stand at a bar in one of the local pubs jotting down notes on the conversation I was having. Walking to, and attending, listing sessions at court were also occasions when the notebook was put away. A researcher does not blend into his background by displaying the symbols of his craft. The policy of recording everything was a reflection of my decision not to ask many questions of the first senior clerk, as I did not want to annoy him. I occasionally made queries, but his explanations were interrupted frequently by telephone calls.

When I transferred to the next set of chambers my method of recording data changed drastically and, to some extent, set the pattern for the future. The senior clerk there criticised me for not asking enough questions, for example, 'Your ignorance [of clerking] is absolute.' He disliked my sitting quietly in the clerks' room taking notes as I had done before, and both he and his junior insisted that I ask questions constantly, irrespective of how busy they appeared, so I badgered them with questions. But I kept my notebook in view and made short notes as necessary.

During this time my dependence on the instantaneous recording of notes was diminishing, and it was possible to hold sequences of events and talk in the memory for subsequent recording. It helped me to be less conspicuous. One clerk said approvingly that I listened and did not talk *too much*. Others would give me a running commentary on what they were doing throughout the day. So the journey back home on the night-time Underground proved an excellent occasion to jot down notes.

Much of the data I collected came through the medium of gossip. Getting oneself plugged into gossip networks is an integral part of any field research. The most sensitive issue I encountered was that of the clerks' income.[10] Zander (1968: 86) underscored their high earnings; in 1968 he quoted figures of senior clerks earning £5,000 to £10,000 a year; Bugler (1976: 28) updated the speculation to £15,000 to £25,000 a year. Nevertheless Zander (1968: 86) admitted, 'There is little hard information about the earnings of the clerks. Even the members of the Chambers frequently do not know what their clerk is earning.'

I was unable to obtain an answer to this question of earnings, except in two cases. One arose from a discussion in a pub with a particularly aggressive clerk who kept hedging on the subject of money. He was teasing me, so to stop the evasion I asked him outright how much he earned. Again he was evasive, but he admitted that it was possible for clerks to be averaging £20,000 a year. In the other case I accompanied a clerk on a visit to a mortgage broker when the clerk was considering buying a country cottage. The broker asked about the clerk's income, which the clerk estimated at £17,000 a year. And it is possible that that sum did not include everything. In the end I must admit I never really cracked the shell of silence that surrounded the question.[11] In contrast to their shyness about their income, several clerks freely offered information about their sex lives.

There is always a problem of reliability when gossip is taken as data. In this situation the researcher is quite powerless to ask for 'the truth'. All he can do is to test each bit of information against other informants' opinions and statements. This rough-and-ready form of triangulation will at least allow one to *feel* whether the information is correct or not.

The demon drink. At this point I want to describe a problem for which I was completely unprepared. On my first day in the Temple the senior and first junior clerks took me to a local pub and bought me two or three pints of beer. So the afternoon went by in a slight haze. The next day was Friday, a special day, when George would meet his friends for an extended, and intensive, drinking session. It was done very smoothly; as each clerk entered the pub he would buy a round of drinks for the others. Occasionally things were reversed, and those already in the pub would buy a round for the newcomer and others. I had eight to ten pints of Guinness bought for me (I can't remember the exact number), and I think I may have drunk six of them. However many it was, the barman commented that it was a shame for me to leave the beer, but I couldn't manage any more. I was becoming aware that fairly large amounts of drink were going to be the norm. It was a daunting prospect. During my period in the field, approximately eight months, my consumption of alcohol in all its forms exceed any previous levels. I was drinking regularly most lunchtimes and several evenings a week. Sometimes a session would go through the whole night; one such lasted twelve hours. The weekends became very valuable—I used them to recover.

Drinking also created other problems, such as when I was banned from a pub with two other clerks. Having drunk a substantial quantity of beer one night, we decided to gatecrash a private party in the rooms above the bar. We successfully negotiated our way in but were spotted by the landlady, who was not on the best of terms with one of my colleagues. She threw us out, and while we were waiting downstairs for a taxi one of them, who was southern Irish, had an argument with the head barman, who was from Northern Ireland, over the serving of drinks after hours. The two nearly had a fight, but fortunately the taxi arrived in time. The following day we heard on the grapevine that we had been banned. At first I was afraid this would cut me off from a profitable area of research, but the damage was not too bad, as that particular pub was already losing most of its clerks to another and the ban only served to accelerate the process. One difficulty arose, however, when later in my research some clerks decided to have a drink at lunchtime and went to that pub. I had to make an excuse at the last minute to avoid embarrassment. Two or three months after the ban had been imposed I was able to return to the pub.

At other times the problems were not so immediate. The night before I was due to lunch with the chairman of the BCA I had had a hectic evening at a club. Consequently I was not at my most alert the next day and had serious doubts about whether I would appear sensible. I concentrated hard and survived the lunch.

It could be thought that I was foolish to get drunk so often (my girlfriend did), but I believe the research would have suffered otherwise. A significant part of legal life revolves around the consumption of alcohol, to have excised it from my fieldwork would have only distorted the picture.

One further point should be made about drink and research. Re-reading notes made when drunk raised some questions about how inebriation affected the quality of my recording. First, I used to have some trouble making my notes, because after drinking I knew at what point on the homeward journey I would become incapable of writing. Second, if I did not make notes fairly soon after the event I might forget some things. Third, there was the difficulty of actually *reading* the notes. Frequently the handwriting was a scrawl. I felt everything was usually there on paper, with only occasional blank spots. Although I have been unable to locate any research that discusses the problems of intoxication during research (most researchers, it appears, don't drink or get intoxicated), I strongly suspect the degree of intoxication to have some effect on the outcome.[12]

Progressing in the field. Through luck I managed to switch into other types of chambers. George invited my girlfriend and me to the BCA annual dinner and dance. After the meal I noticed the chairman circulating among the guests. Although I didn't know him, I introduced myself. Fortunately he had heard of me and invited me to lunch.

He accepted my enquiry seriously, in contrast to the Secretary. Moreover I was well settled in the Temple by this time, and even had he wanted to prevent me from doing research I think he would have had some difficulty. Notwithstanding, he helped me gain access to other chambers. He also provided me with the *Methods Manual for Counsel's Clerks* (BCA, 1970), a *vade mecum* for clerks which nobody appeared to use (it was out of date) and nobody liked (no one was prepared to revise it), and he let me have the BCA annual reports, 1948 to 1976, which provided a great deal of material on the professional aspirations of clerks.

I also found some comparative materials. The chairman put me in touch with a barrister's clerk in Melbourne, Victoria, a state that contains a *de facto* division between barristers and solicitors. There the clerk managed chambers of a hundred barristers, as compared with the English average of fourteen. And he received a percentage.

Nan Wilson's doctoral thesis (1965) on the Scottish Faculty of Advocates mentioned four or five clerks in Edinburgh who clerked the entire faculty, also for a percentage.[13] But the faculty has now converted its clerks into the employees of a company, Faculty Services Ltd.

The most exotic comparison was provided by the Indian *munshi* (Morrison, 1972, 1974), who appeared to be caught in an embittered conflict with his barrister, the *vakil*. Each was continually trying to find ways of defrauding the other of his rightful dues. They were never reconciled, and the struggle was only resolved when the *vakil* attained the ideal of government office.

Through the chairman of the BCA I gained entry to civil, Chancery and revenue chambers. Some of the original clerks I knew objected to my shifting ground into new areas. They thought there was sufficient material to be found among the common law chambers. In one way they were right, but I felt I could not deny myself, or the project, the opportunity to become familiar with lesser-known aspects of clerking. As it turned out, they used to pump me for information about life in other sets. 'Is it very dull in tax chambers?' 'What's so-and-so's business like?'

Other problems. There are fundamental problems: those external to the researcher and those he generates himself. Take the external problems first. I have already outlined the difficulties over access and entry. One further problem only came to my notice during the fieldwork. My status was to some extent a reflection of my credentials, or lack of them. I had started graduate work immediately after taking my law degree: I had not qualified as a barrister or solicitor. To the barristers' clerks this 'unqualification' made me acceptable, less threatening. Had I been a qualified lawyer the research would have been impossible: no one would have talked to me. For example, my girlfriend was studying for the Bar exam while I was doing the fieldwork, and while she was a student clerks would call her by her first name. As soon as she was called to the Bar she became 'Miss ———' to them. A barrister or solicitor is someone a clerk does business with, even when they are drinking together. Being a law graduate, then, freed me from those constraints and allowed me to do the research.

There were, however, adverse reactions to my presence and criticisms about the 'futility' of the study. Some clerks disliked the idea that their almost unknown occupation might be opened up to public view. They constantly emphasised the esoteric, arcane aspects of their job, such as the complexities of having to manage the idiosyncracies of 'twenty-three prima-donnas', as one put it. A number of them concluded that because of their incommensurable individuality I would never be able to generalise about them. One went further and suggested I give up this 'nonsense' and write a novel about clerks instead.

Some barristers also reacted strongly to my presence in their chambers. My visit to a set was usually the result of an agreement between the senior clerk and the head of chambers; the remainder of the barristers would know of me only when they saw me in the clerks' room. For the first day or two they would not notice me and assume I was a solicitor, or solicitor's clerk, or counsel's clerk. They would ignore me except for a casual 'hello'. As my visit lengthened, their curiosity would grow, and they would begin to ask, 'Who's that chap?' Some thought me a representative of the Customs and Excise, investigating barristers' Value Added Tax returns, or a spy for the Royal Commission on Legal Services;[14] perhaps a spy for Michael Zander. Once a senior barrister cross-examined me. A large man, with strong 'presence', he came into the clerks' room. I was the only occupant.

'Who are you?'

'My name is John Flood. I'm doing some research on barristers' clerks.'

'Come to my room a minute. I'd like to talk to you.' We go into his room. There are two other barristers and a pupil there.

'Would you mind leaving us for a moment, chaps? Oh, James' (the pupil), 'could you lend me a couple of cigarettes? . . . Thanks, Sit down. Now, *what* exactly are you doing?'

'I'm trying to describe what barristers' clerks do, and show what part they play in the legal system. I believe they've been unduly criticised on the basis of insubstantial evidence.'

'*Why* are you doing this research?'

'Because I'm interested in the legal profession, and also I'm doing it for my Master's degree at Warwick University.'

The pace of his questions accelerated.

'And *whose* idea was it?'

'It's mine.'

'And what are your qualifications?'

'I hold a law degree.'

'*Where* from?'

Here, perhaps, I was stupid—I told the truth. 'LSE.'

'Are you anything to do with that man Zander?'

'Well . . . he did teach me once.'

'You know the trouble with him, don't you? Everybody knows. He's a failed barrister. So he becomes a solicitor and attacks the Bar. If he got his way and we were nationalised, half or more of the Bar would emigrate. We wouldn't stay here having people like him telling us what to do . . .'

There was a knock on the door and the senior clerk entered.

'Excuse me, sir, I was looking for John. Do you mind if I have him back, sir? We're about to go over the road to check the lists.'

I got up gladly. I was worried how much longer my cross-examination would continue. My nerves were dancing around alarmingly; I was not used to this sort of verbal onslaught. Outside the room the clerk apologised.

'I'd never have let this happen if I'd been there. Don't worry about it. But he's good, isn't he?'

Problems arise, too, from the researcher's proximity to the subjects. The researcher wants to get inside the subject's mind, but how far should he agree with him? For example, Polsky (1967: 135) writes:

Studying a criminal in his natural setting . . . means studying him in *his* usual environs rather than yours, in his living quarters or streets or taverns or wherever, not in your home or your laboratory. And it means you mustn't 'schedule' him, mustn't try to influence his shifting choices among his environments or interfere with his desire either for mobility or immobility. If he wants to sit in front of his TV set and drink beer and watch a ball game for a couple of hours, so do you; if he wants to walk the streets or go bar-hopping, so do you; if he wants to go to the racetrack, so do you; if he indicates (for whatever reason) that it's time for you to get lost, you get lost. (Emphasis in original.)

I think I have shown how far I was prepared to go. But a related problem is that of over-empathy. Research is not just a mechanical activity, it has consequences for oneself. One undergoes changes as one's experience increases. At the start of the project I was heavily influenced by Zander's view that clerks were bad for the legal profession. While doing the field research I attempted to suspend such moral judgements and maintain an objective, open-minded attitude. During the fieldwork some of the relationships developed into friendships, and for a time I found myself become defensive about barristers' clerks. Both New (1956) and Johnson (1975) warn the prospective researcher against over-empathising, as it may distort the collection and presentation of data or, worse, prevent the researcher from ever publishing his results. My own predicament was moving towards this extreme, especially when I became a clerk.

It was a new set of chambers, and I happened to be available. I enjoyed the work, even though the mixture of roles caused some confusion at first. The barristers couldn't decide whether I should be treated as a colleague or a clerk. As time passed, they resolved the issue in favour of me as a clerk. Sometimes, when no one else was around, one would talk to me on equal terms. Nevertheless I had to decide where my loyalties lay. And I decided in favour of my senior clerk, which meant I reported to him the things that he would want to know in order to organise the barristers. The solicitors, because I saw them less frequently, tended to treat me as a clerk.

There were times when I felt like staying on and remaining a clerk. The researcher part of me still functioned, however, and each evening after work I would write up my notes. Among other things, the comments of close friends about my views, behaviour, and the job made me reconsider my situation; they thought I was reneging on my commitment to study clerks because I was becoming one. To them I appeared to subscribe to the clerks' viewpoint. So I took a brief respite from the research and the job. A few months later I returned to those chambers and, as a favour to the senior clerk, worked in them for two weeks; but by then I had realised I didn't want to be a clerk. Perhaps Madge's exhortation (1965: 137) to the researcher demands too much of him or her: 'When the heart of the observer is made to beat as the heart of any other member of the group under observation, rather than as a detached emissary from some distant laboratory, then he has earned the title of *participant-observer.*'

Reactions to research. One of the difficulties inherent in such a work as this is that once it has been written the observer's cover has been blown completely—that is, the observed are now able to read his views. This is an extremely critical moment for him, as most probably he will want to carry out further research (and most research reports emphasise or belabour the point of, the need for, further research—a kind of exemption clause), but his subjects, in effect, know what he is looking for. Moreover, if they are an oversensitive group, as barristers' clerks are, they may withhold future co-operation. It depends on what kind of bargain the researcher has struck with the subjects; if he has *carte blanche,* then he hopes they will respect his freedom; if he has, in Douglas's terms, made an 'unholy alliance' he is put in the position of the 'social investigator [who] cracks the secrecy, but buries the secrets, one by one, in a tomb of silence—as do all the professions which deal with the problems of people' (1976: 43).

During the writing I produced a working paper based on the data I had collected; basically it was a summary (Flood, 1977). I circulated it to some of the clerks for their comments, but only one replied. He had drafted some notes on the working paper and gave me other comments in an interview as well. In the main he did not like my use of clerks' verbatim comments, most of which he considered 'offensive to members of the Bar'. For example, in the case of the quotation about sewing on a barrister's fly button, he would have preferred 'fixing a buckle on to his breeches', something which he once did for one of his Queen's Counsel. As he put it, 'I don't like *fly buttons.*' Perhaps his opinion of me was summarised in one of his written comments (which he meant to remove but did not): 'Quoting what some clerks told him shows what a young man he is, but nevertheless makes better reading.' After the interview we went to the pub for a beer. However, during our third double whisky he began to tell me about the time when he took control of his chambers on the retirement of the previous senior. His first question to the outgoing clerk was 'Have you got any shits in the chambers, [George]?' He told me how he had removed some barristers and replaced them with others. He did not seem to realise he was contradicting himself. But I made no bargains or 'unholy alliances', and I never believed it was necessary to cover up or provide a public relations exercise for them.

During the research process I found participant observation the most congenial method, for a number of reasons. First, the clerks themselves were sympathetic to my role as participant and observer. They had previously expressed some reluctance about the idea of the 'market research' approach.[15] Second, virtually nothing was known about clerks, making it extremely difficult to frame a coherent questionnaire. Third, for such a small group a quantitative study would probably not have produced many useful results. However, in future research, lawyers should be prepared to make use of the many different techniques developed by social scientists. In England, David Podmore's (1980), study of solicitors in the wider community has provided useful guidelines. Among the most promising ideas for the study of legal professions are those of John P. Heinz and Edward O. Laumann in Chicago.[16] Their studies of the Chicago Bar have employed sophisticated statistical techniques that have produced excellent results. The ideal research project will contain a mixture of qualitative and quantitative techniques.

NOTES

1 A note on the meaning of 'ethnography' is in order here. Harold C. Conklin, the Yale anthropologist, defines an ethnographer as 'an anthropologist who attempts—at least in part of his professional work—to record and describe the culturally significant behaviours of a particular society. Ideally, this description, an ethnography, requires a long period of intimate study and residence in a small, well-defined community, knowledge of the spoken language, and the employment of a wide range of observational techniques including prolonged face-to-face contacts with members of the local group, direct participation in some of the group's activities, and a greater emphasis on intensive work with informants than on the use of documentary or survey data. Used nonspecifically, ethnography refers to the discipline concerned with producing such cultural descriptions. [1968: 172–3].

2   At the time of the research, two government commissions had received evidence from the Barristers' Clerks' Association: *First Interim Report of the Committee on County Court Procedures*, Cmnd 7648 (1948); *Final Report of the Committee on Supreme Court Practice and Procedure*, Cmnd 8878 (1953). Later the BCA submitted evidence to Benson (1979) and Oliver and Woolf (1981). The following reports are from commissions and committees that one would have thought would have taken evidence from the BCA but did not: *Report of the Interdepartmental Committee on the Business of the Criminal Courts*, Cmnd 1289 (1961); Beeching (1969); Monopolies (1970); *Report of the Committee on Legal Education*, Cmnd 4595 (1971); *Report of the Committee on the Distribution of Criminal Business*, Cmnd 6323 (1975); *Monopolies and Mergers Commission Report on the Two-counsel Rule*, H.C. 512 (1976); *Commission Report on Restrictions on Advertising by Barristers*, H.C. 559 (1976).

3   Personal communication from A. D. M. Oulton, of the Lord Chancellor's Office.

4   Personal communication from the Clerk to the Faculty of Advocates.

5   One of the most concise and elegant theoretical statements on professionalism is Johnson (1972), though it ignores the symbolic aspects of professionalism, for which see Hughes (1958) and Becker (1970).

6   Abel-Smith and Stevens (1967: x, 239 n. 4, 410 nn. 4, 6).

7   Personal communication from Senior Master Jacob of the Queen's Bench Division.

8   Since the early 1960s Michael Zander, Professor of Law at the London School of Economics and Political Science, has been a critic of the English legal profession and legal system and was, in part, instrumental in bringing the Royal Commission on Legal Services into existence in 1976. He submitted over 700 pages of evidence to the commission. His most trenchant statement is found in Zander (1968).

9   This extract and others are taken from my field notes.

10   See chapter 2.

11   Nor did Benson (1979: II, s. 14).

12   Cf. Bottomley (1978), who reported similar experiences. I should also point out that the clerks did *not* appear adversely affected by the drink.

13   See also Wilson (1968a, 1968b).

14   The establishment of the Royal Commission on Legal Services and my fieldwork coincided.

15   See the low response elicited by the survey on barristers' clerks' incomes commissioned by the Royal Commission on Legal Services (Benson 1979: II, s. 14).

16   Heinz and Laumann (1977, 1978, 1979, 1983).

Appendix 2

SOLICITORS' RESPONSES TO REQUESTS FOR PAYMENT OF COUNSEL'S FEES

I spent one morning in a common law set of chambers telephoning approximately fifteen solicitors' firms to persuade them to pay the outstanding fees of a particular barrister (fairly junior; mostly magistrates' court work, with some appearances in the Crown Court). There were approximately three hundred cases on the list, evenly distributed between the firms. The extremes were represented by one firm with one unpaid fee and two firms owing fees on approximately thirty cases. Each number represents a firm.

1 The case has been on at the magistrates' court, but is now going to the High Court, so no payment yet.
2 No reply.
3 Telephone later, as the staff are too busy to deal with the matter at present.
4 Send a list of fees to be attended to.
5 Sympathetic, but the secretary who deals with fees is on holiday, thus fees will be dealt with in two weeks' time.
6 The files must be searched; promise to telephone chambers later. (Call not returned.)
7 Promise to look up fees and deal with them promptly.
8 Lady who deals with fees away for the week. Return call then.
9 Expressed surprise at notice of unpaid fees. Requested copies of fee notes with promise of payment.
10 Noncommital—'I'll see what I can do.'
11 Promise to telephone next day. (Call not returned.)
12 Helpful. The solicitor explained the state of affairs: the Old Bailey case had been taxed, the solicitor had received his cheque, therefore the barrister should receive his soon; still waiting for the Inner London Crown Court cheque; promise to return call the next day on the magistrates' court case. (Call not returned.)
13 The receptionist could not locate a partner who would be able to assist. The litigation partner proper on holiday, but another might be able to handle the problem. Promise to telephone later. (Call not returned.)
14 The case was not the responsibility of the London office; telephone [a provincial town].

Next day:

2   Reasonably helpful. All outstanding fees were being settled, and a cheque should be received at the end of the month or beginning of the next.
14 Solicitor at provincial town office was helpful. The bill had been taxed, waiting for cheque from the local Crown court.
15 Expressed surprise at unpaid fees: 'We usually pay on the return of the brief.' Requested details of the cases as the files could not be located. Promised to pay.
16 Indifferent. Noted details of cases over the telephone. 'If you don't hear from me in two weeks, get in touch, I'll look into it.'

Approximately a third of the firms paid the outstanding fees. Notably, those with the largest number of unpaid fees did not settle their accounts. The clerk, however, declined to report them to the Law Society.

Appendix 3

BCA EXAMINATION PAPERS

The examination for qualified membership of the BCA is divided into two parts. There must be an interval of three years between taking Part I and taking Part II. The following papers were set in 1981.

Part I

SECTION 1   Time suggested: 30 minutes
Maximum marks: 10 for each question

1 You are writing to:
   (a) a High Court Judge,
   (b) a Circuit Judge,
   (c) a High Court Master,
   (d) a Registrar,
   (e) a Recorder.
  How would you commence your letter?
2 Name the Inns of Court who currently 'Call to the Bar.'
3 After what period of time may
   (a) a pupil accept instructions to act from a Solicitor?
   (b) a practising Barrister accept a pupil?
4 List the steps to be taken when Counsel asks you to fix a conference in which he holds papers.
5 Define 'a Tort'.

SECTION 2   Suggested time: 1 hour
Maximum marks as shown against each question

6 Indicate by drawing a form of DIARY PAGE you believe to be the most beneficial for Counsel's Chambers and explain how you can relate it to an accounting system. (20)
7 Write what you know about the fixing of cases before:
   (a) The Queen's Bench Division,
   (b) Chancery Division (Witness List),
   (c) The Official Referee.
8 Write a short essay on 'The Knights Templar'. (20)
9 The trial of Regina *v.* Hither is to be heard before the Beddington Crown Court sitting in the Civic Centre Complex, Beddington, Beddingshire.

Your Counsel, Mr Keen N. Active, is instructed for the Defence. Mr Ian A. Sleep acts for the Prosecution.

The trial is for alleged offences against the Obscene Publications Act and it is necessary for both Counsel to view prior to trial certain films held in police possession.

It is necessary for a fixture to be obtained because Defence witnesses are coming from Sweden.

Mr Sleep's Clerk has indicated that Mr Sleep and the Prosecution generally are available for this 3 day trial between the dates of 7th to 18th December inclusive.

Your Mr Active is only available between the 2nd to 10th December inclusive.

Both Counsel are available for a 2 hour view of the films on 25th November at 2.00 p.m.

(a) Write a letter to the Listing Officer at Beddington Crown Court seeking a fixture.

(b) Write a letter to Inspector Yardbird of the Beddington County Constabulary, The Police H.Q., Peel Lane, Beddington, seeking an appointment for both Counsel to view the films. (50)

10 Write what you know to be the correct procedure and timing of 'returning a brief'. (30)

Part II

SECTION 1 *Time suggested: 20 minutes*
Maximum marks: 5 for each question

Please answer ALL the questions in this section. Brief but accurate answers are required.

1 In which year was it that legislation permitting effective control of land was passed?
2 Who is Terry Rayson and what are his duties?
3 What is an Order 14 Summons in the Queen's Bench Division?
4 What is a 'Special Procedure' case in the Family Division?
5 What is the time limit for appealing to the Commissioners of Inland Revenue against a tax assessment?
6 Under what circumstances is a Petition for leave to appeal to the House of Lords necessary?
7 Name five forms of action that can be commenced in the County Court.
8 What is an Indictment?
9 Name the Inns of Court who 'Call to the Bar'.
10 What is the difference between a Solicitor's 'Articled Clerk' and a Barrister's 'Pupil'?

SECTION 2 *Time suggested: 1 hour 20 minutes Maximum marks: 25 each*

11 Write what you know of Chancery Motions. In particular, give details

of the documentation served on the Defendant, the days upon which Motions are heard and the reason why so many Motions are stood over for a short period of time.

12   Give a general outline, starting with the issue of the Writ, of the course of Queen's Bench action to judgement.

13   Give a description of the work of the Family Division Divisional Court.

14   Detail the full appeal processes from a County Court Registrar through to the House of Lords.

15   Give a summary of the 'No Local Bar' rules.

16   Explain what is known in Criminal cases from the words:
(a) Section 1.
(b) Section 2.
(c) Section 7.
(d) Section 28.
(e) Section 29.

17   (a) What are the Leap Frog provisions in Tax cases and when could they come into operation?
(b) Set out the procedure for obtaining a Planning permission.
(c) Detail the mode of hearing of proceedings at the Patent Office.

18   Write a concise history of the area known as 'The Temple and Lincoln's Inn' combined with some notes on the present structure and organisation of 'The Bar'.

SECTION 3   Time suggested: 1 hour 20 minutes   Maximum marks: 25 each

19   Counsel appeared for the Defence in the Hamminster Crown Court in the case of R. *v.* R. I. Amour. The case had but one count on the indictment of G.B.H. The prosecution were calling 7 witnesses (18 pages of statements) to prove their case. The Defendant had 5 witnesses (including the Defendant). There was a conflict on the medical evidence necessitating the calling of Doctors on both sides. On the morning of the fixed date for trial the Defendant changed his instructions to a plea of guilty. The hearing of the plea lasted 1 hour. Counsel has spent 4 hours in general preparation and had 2 conferences pre-trial (one with the Doctor). The conferences lasted 1 hour each. Hamminster is 50 miles from the nearest centre for the Bar.

On taxation the sum of £50 Brief and £10 Conferences was allowed. Set out the processes through to final appeal to the Supreme Court Taxing Master seeking a review of this Legal Aid fee.

20   Set out, using illustrations if necessary, the method and form of keeping a record of Counsel's Fees from the time when instructions are received to the issue of a V.A.T. receipted invoice.

21   Write a short essay on the subject of assessing a Brief fee.

22   A diary is an essential feature in the maintenance of a record of Court and Conference work to be done.

Indicate a form of diary and other aids which assist in the recording of such work and the manner in which it can be linked to the accounting system.

BIBLIOGRAPHY

REPORTS AND CASES

Beeching, Lord (1969), *Report of the Royal Commission on Assizes and Quarter Sessions, 1966–69,* Cmnd 4153 HMSO, London.
Benson, Sir Henry (1979), *Final Report of the Royal Commission on Legal Services* (2 vols.), Cmnd 7648, HMSO, London.
Evershed, Lord (1953), *Final Report on Supreme Court Practice and Procedure,* Cmnd 8878, HMSO, London.
Monopolies Commission (1970), *Report on the General Effect on the Public Interest of Certain Restrictive Practices so far as they Prevail in Relation to the Supply of Professional Services,* Cmnd 4463, HMSO, London.
Oliver, Lord Justice, and Woolf, J. M. (1981), *Report of the Review Body on the Chancery Division of the High Court,* Cmnd 8205, HMSO, London.
Annual Reports of the Bar Committee; Annual Statements of the General Council of the Bar; Annual Statements of the Senate of the Inns of Court and the Bar, 1884–76.
Barristers' Clerks' Association Annual Reports, 1949–76.
Ex parte Cotton (1846) 9 Beav. 107.
Lyster *v.* Spearman (1882) 12 L.T. Jo. 391; 3 Digest (Repl.) 360.

BOOKS AND ARTICLES

Abel-Smith, Brian, and Stevens, Robert (1967), *Lawyers and the Courts. A Sociological Study of the English Legal System, 1750–1965,* Heinemann Educational, London.
Abel-Smith, Brian, and Stevens, Robert (1968), *In Search of Justice. Society and the Legal System,* Allen Lane, The Penguin Press, London.
Aylett, Sydney (1978), *Under the Wigs,* Eyre Methuen, London.
Bankowski, Zenon, and Mungham, Geoffrey (1976), *Images of Law,* Routledge & Kegan Paul.
Bar Council (1974), *The Machinery of Fee Collection,* General Council of the Bar, London.
Barristers' Clerks' Association (1970), *A Methods Manual for Counsel's Clerks,* Barristers' Clerks' Association, London.
Becker, Howard S. (1970), 'The nature of a profession', *Sociological Work.*

Method and Substance, Allen Lane, The Penguin Press, London, pp. 87–103.

Becker, Howard S., and Carper, J. W. (1956), 'The development of identification with an occupation', *American Journal of Sociology,* LXI, pp. 289–98.

Blok, A. (1969), 'Variations in patronage', *Sociologische Gids,* XVI, pp. 365–78.

Blumberg, Abraham S. (1967), 'The practice of law as a confidence game: organisational co-optation of a profession', *Law and Society Review,* I, pp. 15–39.

Boissevain, Jeremy (1966), 'Patronage in Sicily', *Man* (N.S.), I, pp. 18–33.

Boissevain, Jeremy (1974), *Friends of Friends. Networks, Manipulators and Coalitions,* Basil Blackwell, Oxford.

Bottomley, Bill (1978), 'Words, deeds and postgraduate research', *Inside the Whale. Ten Personal Accounts of Social Research,* ed. Colin Bell and Sol Encel, Pergamon Press, Rushcutters Bay, Australia, pp. 216–37.

Boulton, Sir William (1975), *A Guide to Conduct and Etiquette at the Bar of England and Wales* (6th ed.), Butterworth, London.

Bowker, A. E. (1947), *Behind the Bar,* Staples Press, London.

Bowker, A. E. (1961), *A Lifetime with the Law,* W. H. Allen, London.

Brickman, Lester (1971), 'Expansion of the lawyering process through a new delivery system: the emergence and state of legal para-professionalism', *Columbia Law Review,* LXXI, pp. 1153–255.

Bugler, Jeremy (1976), 'NCOs of the law', *New Statesman,* 5 March, pp. 286–7.

Caplan, Jonathan (1978), 'The criminal bar', *The Bar on Trial,* Quartet Books, London, pp. 130–47.

Carlen, Pat (1975), 'Magistrates' courts: a game theoretic analysis', *Sociological Review* (N.S.), XXIII, pp. 347–79.

Carlen, Pat (1976), *Magistrates' Justice,* Law in Society series, Martin Robertson, London.

Conklin, Harold C. (1968), 'Ethnography', *International Encyclopedia of the Social Sciences,* V, ed. David L. Sills, Macmillan and Free Press, New York, pp. 172–8.

Cooper, Eric W. (n.d.), 'An introduction to the role of the barrister's clerk', unpublished paper.

Daniell, Timothy (1971), *Inns of Court,* Wildy & Sons, London.

Douglas, Jack D. (1976), *Investigative Social Research. Individualised and Team Research,* Russell Sage, Beverley Hills, Cal.

Edwards, J. Ll. J. (1964), *The Law Officers of the Crown,* Sweet & Maxwell, London.

Endacott, R. R. (1975), 'Systemization and the legal assistant in the law office', *Nebraska Law Review,* LIV, pp. 46–57.

Flood, John A. (1977), 'Barristers' clerks', *Warwick Law Working Papers,* No. 2, reprinted (1979) in *Journal of the Legal Profession,* IV, pp. 23–39.

Foster, Ken (1973), 'The location of solicitors', *Modern Law Review,* XXXVI, pp. 153–66.

Fry, W. R. (1973), 'A short review of the paralegal movement', *Clearinghouse Review,* VII, pp. 463–9.

Garfinkel, Harold (1967), *Studies in Ethnomethodology*, Prentice-Hall, Englewood Cliffs, N.J.

Gluckman, Max (1968), 'Psychological, sociological and anthropological explanations of witchcraft and gossip: a clarification', *Man* (N.S.), III, pp. 20–34.

Goffman, Erving (1952), 'On cooling the mark out', *Journal of Personality and Social Psychology*, XXV, pp. 451–63.

Goffman, Erving (1956), 'The nature of deference and demeanor', *American Anthropologist*, LVIII, pp. 473–502.

Goffman, Erving (1959), *The Presentation of Self in Everyday Life*, Penguin, Harmondsworth.

Goffman, Erving (1964), 'The neglected situation', *American Anthropologist*, LXVI, pp. 133–6; reprinted in (1972) *Language and Social Context*, ed. P. Giglioli, Penguin, Harmondsworth.

Gower, L. C. B. (1963), 'Review of Megarry, *Lawyer and Litigant in England*', *International and Comparative Law Quarterly*, XII, pp. 1079–86.

Graham-Green, Graham J. (1973), *Criminal Costs and Legal Aid*, Butterworth, London.

Hall, Oswald (1948), 'Stages of a medical career', *American Journal of Sociology*, LIII, pp. 327–36.

Halsbury (1973), 'Barristers', *Halsbury's Laws of England*, III, (4th ed.), Butterworth, London.

Handelman, Don (1973), 'Gossip in encounter: the transmission of information in a bounded social setting', *Man* (N.S.) VIII, pp. 210–27.

Harrison, C. B. (n.d.), 'Fees and other accounting for the barrister's clerk', unpublished paper.

Hazard, Jr., Geoffrey C. (1965), 'Reflections on four studies of the legal profession', *Social Problems* (summer supplement: *Law and Society*), XII, pp. 46–54.

Hazell, Robert (1978a), 'Pupilage', *The Bar on Trial*, ed. Robert Hazell, Quartet Books, London, pp. 82–98.

Hazell, Robert (1978b), 'Clerks and fees', *The Bar on Trial*, ed. Robert Hazell, Quartet Books, London, pp. 99–129.

Hazell, Robert (ed.) (1978c), *The Bar on Trial*, Quartet Books, London.

Heinz, John P., *et al.* (1976), 'Diversity, representation and leadership in an urban bar: a first report on a survey of the Chicago bar', *American Bar Foundation Research Journal*, 1976, pp. 717–85.

Heinz, John P., and Laumann, Edward O. (1977), 'Specialisation and prestige in the legal profession: the structure of deference', *American Bar Foundation Research Journal*, 1977, pp. 155–216.

Heinz, John P., and Laumann, Edward O. (1978), 'The legal profession: client interests, professional roles and social hierarchies', *Michigan Law Review*, LXXVI, pp. 1111–42.

Heinz, John P., and Laumann, Edward O. (1979), 'The organisation of lawyers' work: size, intensity, and co-practice of the fields of law', *American Bar Foundation Research Journal*, 1979, pp. 217–46.

Heinz, John P., and Laumann, Edward O. (1983), *Chicago Lawyers. The Professions of the Bar*, American Bar Foundation, Chicago, and Russell Sage Foundation, New York.

Holdsworth, Sir William (1966), *A History of English Law*, Methuen and Sweet & Maxwell, London.

Homans, George C. (1958), 'Social behaviour as exchange', *American Journal of Sociology*, LXIII, pp. 59–60.

Hughes, Everett C. (1958), 'Work and self', *Men and their Work*, Free Press, Glencoe, Ill., pp. 42–55.

Hughes, Everett C. (1971), 'Good people and dirty work', *The Sociological Eye. Selected Papers on Work, Self and the Study of Society*, Aldine-Atherton, Chicago, pp. 87–97.

Hyde, H. Montgomery (1964), *Norman Birkett*, Hamish Hamilton, London.

Jacob, I. H., *et al.* (1979), *The Supreme Court Practice*, Butterworth, Stevens and Sweet & Maxwell, London.

Johnson, John M. (1975), *Doing Field Research*, Free Press, New York.

Johnson, Terence J. (1972), *Professions and Power*, Macmillan, London.

Johnstone, Quintin, and Flood, John A. (1982), 'Paralegals in English and American law offices', *Windsor Yearbook of Access to Justice*, II, pp. 152–90.

Johnstone, Quintin, and Hopson, Jr., Dan (1967), *Lawyers and their Work. An Analysis of the Legal Profession in the United States and England*, Bobbs-Merrill, Indianapolis.

Kellner, Peter, and Crowther-Hunt, Lord (1980), *The Civil Servants. An Inquiry into Britain's Ruling Class*, Macdonald, London.

Kennedy, Helena (1978), 'Women at the Bar', *The Bar on Trial*, ed. Robert Hazell, Quartet Books, London, pp. 148–62.

Lamb, Charles (1903), 'The old Benchers of the Inner Temple', *The Essays of Elia*, ed. William Macdonald, Dent, London, pp. 166–84.

Lewis, Philip (1976), 'Defamation: reputation and encounter', *Jahrbuch für Rechtssoziologie und Rechtstheorie*, IV, pp. 271–84.

Lukes, Steven (1974), *Power. A Radical View*, Macmillan, London.

Madge, John (1965), *The Tools of Social Science. An Analytical Description of Social Science Techniques*, Doubleday, Anchor Books, Garden City, N.Y.

Megarry, Robert E. (1962), *Lawyer and Litigant in England*, Stevens, London.

Mills, C. Wright (1940), 'Situated actions and vocabularies of motive', *American Sociological Review*, V, pp. 904–13.

Morrison, Charles (1972), '*Munshis* and their masters: the organisation of an occupational relationship in the Indian legal system', *Journal of Asian Studies*, XXXI, pp. 309–29.

Morrison, Charles (1974), 'Clerks and clients: paraprofessional roles and cultural identities in Indian litigation', *Law and Society Review*, IX, pp. 39–61.

New, Peter Kong-Ming (1956), 'The personal identification of the interviewer', *American Journal of Sociology*, LX, p. 213.

Newland, Sydney G. (1970), *The Barrister's Clerk*, Barristers' Clerks' Association, London.

Paine, Robert (1967), 'What is gossip about? An alternative hypothesis', *Man* (N.S.), II, pp. 278–85.

Podmore, David (1980), *Solicitors and the Wider Community*, Cambridge Studies in Criminology, Heinemann Educational, London.

Poe, Edgar Allan (1978), 'The man of the crowd', *Collected Works of Edgar Allan Poe,* II, ed. Thomas Olive Mabbott, The Bellknap Press of Harvard University Press, Cambridge, Mass., and London, pp. 506–15.

Polsky, Ned (1967), *Hustlers, Beats and Others,* Aldine, Chicago.

Prest, Wilfred R. (1972), *The Inns of Court under Elizabeth I and the Early Stuarts, 1590–1640,* Longman, London.

Reisman, W. Michael (1979), *Folded Lies. Bribery, Crusades, and Reforms,* Free Press, New York.

Roth, Julius A. (1963), *Timetables. Structuring the Passage of Time in Hospital Treatment and other Careers,* Bobbs-Merrill, Indianapolis.

Sachs, Albie, and Wilson, Joan H. (1978), *Sexism and the Law. A Study of Male Beliefs and Legal Bias in Britain and the United States,* Law in Society series, Martin Robertson, London.

Senate of the Inns of Court and the Bar (1980), *Code of Conduct for the Bar of England and Wales,* Senate of the Inns of Court and the Bar, London.

Shibutani, Tamotsu (1955), 'Reference groups as perspectives', *American Journal of Sociology,* LXI, pp. 562–9.

Shibutani, Tamotsu (1962), 'Reference groups and social control', *Human Behaviour and Social Processes. An Interactionist Approach,* ed. Arnod M. Rose, Routledge & Kegan Paul, London, pp. 128–47.

Simon, J. E. S. (1965), 'Review of Edwards, *Law Officers of the Crown'*, *Law Quarterly Review,* LXXXI, pp. 289–96.

Stone, Gregory P. (1962), 'Appearance and the self', *Human Behaviour and Social Processes. An Interactionist Approach,* ed. Arnold M. Rose, Routledge & Kegan Paul, London, pp. 86–118.

Surtees, Robert Smith (1911), *Handley Cross,* Methuen, London.

Thorne, Samuel E. (1959) 'The early history of the Inns of Court, with special reference to Gray's Inn', *Graya,* No. 50, pp. 79–97.

Trollope, Anthony (1956), *Orley Farm,* Oxford University Press, London.

Turner, Ralph H. (1954), 'Role-taking, role standpoint, and reference-group behavior,' *American Journal of Sociology,* LX, pp. 316–28.

Twining, William L. (1973), 'Llewellyn and Hoebel: a case study in inter-disciplinary collaboration', *Law and Society Review,* VII, pp. 561–83, reprinted in (1981), *Law and Social Enquiry. Case Studies of Research,* Studies of Law in Social Change and Development, ed. Robin Luckham, Scandinavian Institute of African Studies and International Center for Law in Development, Uppsala and New York.

Urry, John (1973), *Reference Groups and the Theory of Revolution,* Routledge & Kegan Paul, London.

Walker, R. J. (1980), *Walker and Walker. The English Legal System* (5th ed.), Butterworth, London.

Warren, Nicholas (1978), 'The Inns of Court', *The Bar on Trial,* ed. Robert Hazell, Quartet Books, London, pp. 38–67.

Whyte, William Foot (1955), *Street Corner Society. The Social Structure of an Italian Slum* (2nd ed., enl.), University of Chicago Press, Chicago.

Wickenden, C. D. (1975), *The Modern Family Solicitor. Guidelines for Practice Today and Tomorrow,* Stevens, London.

Wilson, Nan (1965), 'The Sociology of a Profession: The Faculty of

Advocates', unpublished Ph.D. thesis, Edinburgh University.

Wilson, Nan (1968a), 'The professional community: the Edinburgh advocates', *Record of the Association of the Bar of the City of New York*, XXIII, pp. 174–84.

Wilson, Nan (1968b), 'The Scottish Bar: the evolution of the Faculty of Advocates in its historical social setting', *Louisiana Law Review*, XXVIII, pp. 235–57.

Zander, Michael (1968), *Lawyers and the Public Interest*, Weidenfeld & Nicolson, London.

Zander, Michael (1978), *Legal Services for the Community*, Temple Smith, London.

MISCELLANEOUS

Bar List of the United Kingdom 1981, ed. Stevens Editorial Staff, Stevens, London.

Debate on the Second Reading of the Supreme Court Officers (Pensions) Bill (1954), 526 Parl. Deb. H.C. (5th ser.) cols. 1892–932.

Simon's Taxes (1970) (3rd ed.), Butterworth, London, Div. C, pp. 343–4.

INDEX